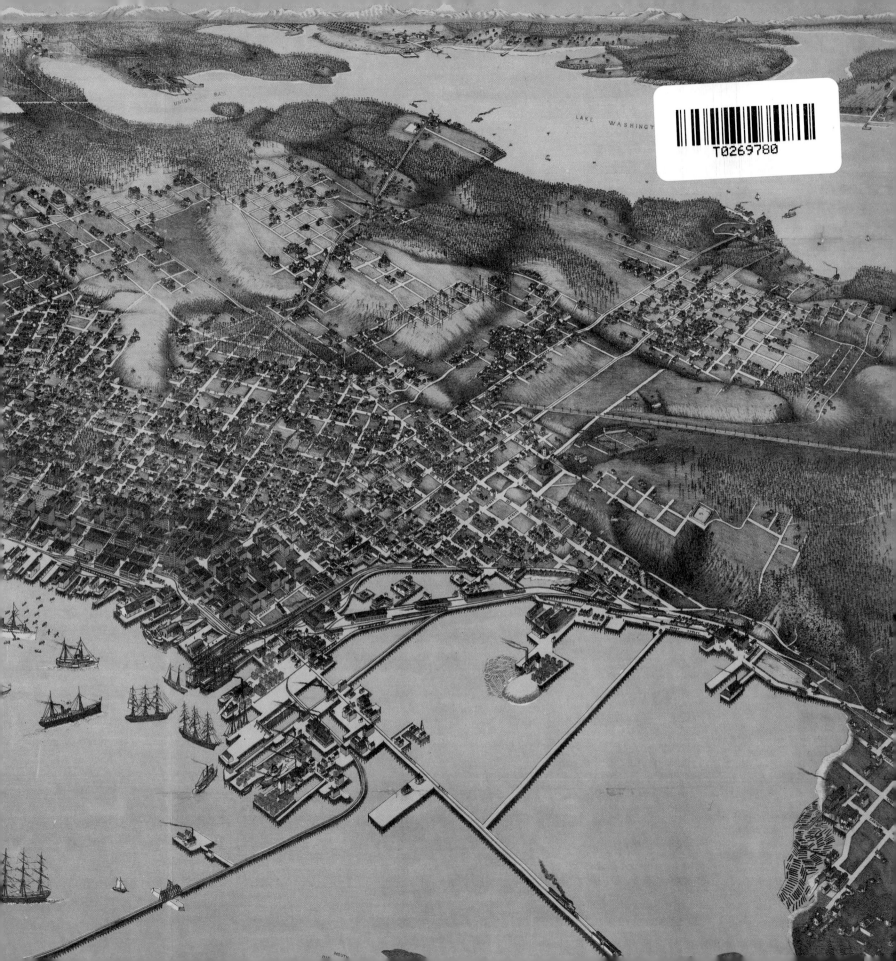

LAKE WASHINGTON

UNION BAY

THE STORY OF THE PORT OF SEATTLE

RISING TIDES AND TAILWINDS

SECOND EDITION

Casey McNerthney, Kit Oldham, and Peter Blecha

HistoryLink / Documentary Media
Seattle, WA

Rising Tides and Tailwinds: The Story of the Port of Seattle

Second Edition (SEA airport 75 edition)
Printed in USA

Produced by HistoryLink and Documentary Media

HistoryLink
admin@historylink.org
www.historylink.org
(206) 447-8140

Documentary Media LLC
books@docbooks.com
www.documentarymedia.com
(206) 935-9292

Port of Seattle production team: Kathy Roeder and Devlin Donnelly
Authors: Casey McNerthney (First Edition: Kit Oldham and Peter Blecha)
Design: Paul Langland Design (First Edition: Nancy Kinnear)
Editing: Tori Smith (First Edition: Tom Brown and Charles Smyth)
Editorial Director: Petyr Beck

ISBN 978-1-933245-71-3

Distributed by the University of Washington Press
uwapress@uw.edu

Library of Congress Control Number: 2024933578

CONTENTS

FOREWORD

by Senator Patty Murray

Senator Patty Murray

Like just about everyone in Washington state, the Port of Seattle is personal to me.

I remember watching the boats go in and out of the harbor as a little girl, some of them perhaps carrying goods we stocked at the five-and-ten-cent store where my dad worked. It's a sight I've seen countless times from ferries on the water, from parks on the waterfront, and from plane windows flying in and out of SEA Airport. I can tell you: it never gets old, and it looks spectacular from every angle.

This book gives us yet another incredible perspective on our waterfront, the Port, SEA Airport, and its legacy — a historical one. And much like the views, the history is wonderfully rich. In 2024, we also mark the 75th anniversary of SEA—an airport that has grown along with our region, and today is as busy as it's ever been.

SEA Airport is a special place. It is where families meet or are reunited. It's where visitors from around the world start and end their trips to Seattle. It's where many begin new lives in the Pacific Northwest. And it's the workplace for tens of thousands of individuals who keep our operations moving.

It is the always-open facility that helps companies thrive and has helped Seattle become the nation's fastest growing city, year after year.

As noted in the introduction to the first edition of this book, "The history of Seattle is to a great extent the history of its waterfront." In telling the story of the Port of Seattle, this book touches on so many other aspects of the history of the city. There are the lumber mills that helped build American cities along the Pacific Coast. There are the fortune seekers heading to Alaska in search of gold and to Asia in pursuit of trade. There are the vacationers who set out for a cruise. There are the service members who set out to protect our country. There are the stories of workers and unions who fought for better conditions, businesses that grew into global ventures, and the hardships they all faced like the Great Depression, the 2008 Financial Crisis, and the COVID pandemic. And of course, there are the Tribes who have been here since time immemorial, and the wildlife that has lived here longer than anyone.

In the early 1940s, when commercial aviation was in its infancy and the idea of a costly airport wasn't always popular, the Port of Seattle stepped up to provide the planning and financial backing to build the airport. SEA Airport has played a critical role in growing this region's economy ever since. From its first day, to the 1962 Seattle World's Fair, to planning for the 2026 FIFA World Cup, SEA Airport has kept pace with our changing region for 75 years. That's because of the people working together each day – in jobs large and small – to make SEA a five-star airport for the next 75 years and beyond.

The Port of Seattle was itself an innovation born of necessity—it was the first public port established through legislation. At the time, it was created to address the problem of a sprawling mess of railroads and private interests crowding the waterfront. Since it was founded over a century ago, the Port has demonstrated the wisdom of establishing a public steward of the city's harbor and working waterfront. The Port is accountable to the people of King County and is rooted in their shared values. It has reliably prioritized the needs and future of the region over short-term profits. Whether it be fostering trade through the Northwest Seaport Alliance, preparing for war, expanding air travel, building a tourism industry through record-setting cruise terminals, serving a growing city, protecting the environment, or addressing the climate crisis, the Port has met the demands of the moment with the public interest at heart. It's a theme you will see time and again throughout this book.

The Port of Seattle remains one of the few port authorities in the nation to oversee both air and seaports. This history does an excellent job tracing what is woven together to make the port, the airport, and Seattle what they are today. It also offers a valuable reminder of what an enduring gift it is to have a public port that can find balance meeting the needs of everyone in our community.

So, you can see why I was delighted to have the chance to write this introduction—and why I am proud to support the Port of Seattle's efforts to serve Washington state communities when I go to work in our nation's capitol. Because, for over a century, the Port hasn't just helped boats, planes, goods, and people navigate the waterfront—it has helped Seattle, King County, their businesses, and their families navigate the challenges of the moment and steer toward a brighter future.

INTRODUCTION

The history of Seattle is to a great extent the history of its waterfront. From the time of its founding by settlers who arrived by water and supported themselves selling timber to passing ships, Seattle has depended more than most cities on waterborne commerce. The city grew up where it did because of the great natural harbor of Elliott Bay, and in its first decades much of the commercial center was built literally in that harbor, on piers and fill rising over muddy tide water.

For more than a century, Seattle's waterfront history has both shaped and been shaped by the Port of Seattle, the independent government body created in 1911 to develop public wharves, piers, waterways, and other harbor facilities essential to the region's trade-dependent economy.

While the Port was created in response to unhappiness with existing harbor conditions, its role and influence have reached far beyond the waterfront. The Port of Seattle regularly expanded and upgraded, and continues to innovate at SEA Airport, known as Sea-Tac in its earlier days. It is a driver of $22.5 billion in regional business revenue that has repeatedly been named North America's best airport. The growth of SEA has parallelled the rise of the companies that Seattle is now known for. If you counted just the number of travelers, the airport's daily traffic would be equivalent to Washington's third largest city.

If the Port of Seattle did not already exist, it is hard to imagine that a government agency could be created today to own and manage the region's major airport, a leading maritime port, Fishermen's Terminal, Shilshole Bay Marina, and the many other facilities that collectively create thousands of jobs and pump billions of dollars into the regional economy. Indeed, the idea that a publicly run port should build and operate Seattle's harbor facilities was controversial a century ago. However, in 1911, progressive reformers, far-sighted civil engineers, and eventually much of the city's political and business elite joined forces to wrest control of the harbor from the private railroad and shipping corporations that dominated it.

impact. SEA Airport more than doubled its International Arrivals capacity and had more than a million travelers use the industry leading Spot Saver program. Billions in other projects are planned for the years ahead—done with a focus on equity, diversity, inclusion, and land stewardship principles.

Of course, there have been challenges over the decades: false starts, missteps, controversies. The first port commissioners faced withering policy criticism until their vision was vindicated by the Port's astounding success during World War I. Sometimes-violent conflicts between labor and management rocked the docks for decades before more cooperative relations were forged between unions, the Port, and private employers. Today, with SEA Airport now holding the smallest geographic area of any major airport in the country, the need for another major airport—and the challenge of finding that ideal space—is inevitable.

But as the Port continues to thrive in its second century, and as SEA Airport celebrates its 75th Anniversary, we recognize that Seattle and the surrounding region would be dramatically different today if not for those who created the Port of Seattle a century ago. As *The Seattle Times* editorial board noted, Washington is the fourth largest exporter of goods thanks in no small part to the Port of Seattle. And with the forward thinking of SEA staff, "Seattle should be proud to have such an airport."

In its first century, the Port readied Seattle for the huge increase in Pacific trade that accompanied World War I; helped the area weather the Great Depression; undertook the task of building and managing Sea-Tac Airport when other agencies did not; made Seattle one of the first West Coast ports to invest in containerized shipping, which revolutionized and vastly expanded Washington's international trade; and more recently has worked to address some of the region's more intractable environmental problems.

The last decade saw creation of the Northwest Seaport Alliance, the marine cargo operating partnership between Seattle and Tacoma—the first of its kind in North America. Port cruise terminals continue to set records for economic

Aerial perspective of Seattle, 1878.

Chapter 1: **BIRTH OF THE PORT**

Water routes and railroads built Seattle. But in the early 1900s, 50 years after the city's founding, the central waterfront — the critical juncture between water and rail — was a chaotic mess. Competing private railroads dominated the waterfront, a tangle of multiple rail lines, terminals, switches, and spurs leading to a confusion of mostly small, privately owned docks, warehouses, mills, and canneries built on wooden pilings over the muddy tide flats of Elliott Bay. Front Street (today's 1st Avenue), running along the shore just inland of the high-tide line, no longer fronted the water. Three more roadways — Post Alley, Western Avenue, and Railroad Avenue (today's Alaskan Way) — paralleled Front Street to the west, running for much of their length offshore, their wood-plank surfaces raised above tide level on log pilings.

The key battleground was the aptly named Railroad Avenue, the outermost street, occupied by eight, and in places nine, separate lines of track that divided Seattle, physically and legally, from its all-important waterfront. From Railroad Avenue's western, waterward side, a fringe of piers and wharves reached out into the harbor. The lifeblood of the

OPPOSITE: Ships bound for Alaska or California were loaded with coal delivered by rail from mines east of Lake Washington, ca 1889.

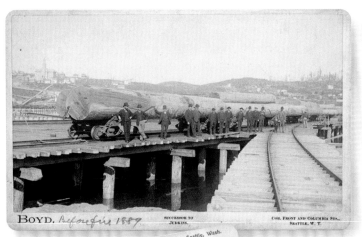

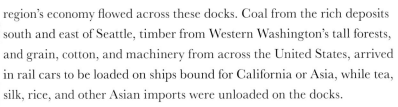

region's economy flowed across these docks. Coal from the rich deposits south and east of Seattle, timber from Western Washington's tall forests, and grain, cotton, and machinery from across the United States, arrived in rail cars to be loaded on ships bound for California or Asia, while tea, silk, rice, and other Asian imports were unloaded on the docks.

Puget Sound's famed Mosquito Fleet of small independently owned steamers also called at the Railroad Avenue piers. Along with providing the primary passenger transportation around the Sound, the fleet carried commercial goods to outlying communities and brought fresh produce from the region's farms to market in Seattle. Across Railroad Avenue from the docks, Western Avenue was lined with commission houses — warehouses where middlemen bought and resold the fresh produce that arrived daily.

However, reaching or even seeing the wharves and water from the produce warehouses and the central city beyond was not easy. Freight cars unloading or switching tracks frequently blocked views and access. Actually traversing Railroad Avenue's 150-foot width and multiple tracks by foot or horse-drawn cart was even more challenging. For pedestrians or horse teams dodging trains and bouncing over rails, the perilous journey was made worse by the often-decrepit wooden road surface. Planks were splintered or rotten, and there were more than a few "man traps" — holes through which the unwary could fall into the cesspool of rotting filth and garbage accumulated among the pilings below.

For many, Railroad Avenue's legal status was just as appalling as (and indeed a major cause of) its physical condition. Three large private corporations — the Great Northern Railway, the Northern Pacific Railroad, and the Pacific Coast Company, which mined the large coalfields in south King County and engaged in coastal trade — owned the tracks and most of the docks and warehouses that lined Railroad Avenue. This fractured private ownership posed barriers to waterfront access and trade every bit as great as the iron rails, lines of box cars, and rotten planks.

Because the railroad companies also owned the piers and warehouses, they controlled wharf availability and rates, which they arranged to serve their own interest in filling trains with cargo, rather than to promote trade and make it easier for the area's farmers and merchants to export and import goods. Beyond that, with competing track and dock owners pursuing their own separate interests, coordinated development of needed new facilities, or just improvement of existing ones, was difficult to achieve. For instance, few of the many piers were large enough to accommodate big oceangoing ships.

With the 1914 opening of the Panama Canal approaching, Seattle (like all West Coast port cities) expected a huge jump in international trade that would boost the local economy. However, city leaders saw little sign that the railroads were preparing the waterfront to meet the demands of this anticipated trade boom. As frustration grew over the railroads' legal and physical stranglehold on Seattle's waterfront, so did pressure for the formation of a publicly owned and operated port.

COURTED AND SPURNED

The problems facing the waterfront that inspired calls for a public port were rooted in both the natural history of Elliott Bay and the human history of the young city on the bay's eastern shore. Seattle was a commercial port city from its founding in 1851. In Elliott Bay, Seattle had one of the world's great deepwater ports, a large protected harbor in which even the biggest ships could anchor close to shore, as the Denny party's clothesline-and-horseshoe sounding demonstrated. But, before the massive reshaping of the land that created today's waterfront, the shore rose sharply from the water's edge with little adjacent dry flat land for commercial or industrial development. Like the Lushootseed-speaking inhabitants of

dʼidʼəlálič ("Little Place Where One Crosses Over") before them, the first settlers clustered on Piner's Point, a low spit projecting into the bay near the south end of today's downtown at Pioneer Square. From that point north, for the entire length of the present central waterfront and beyond to Smith Cove (the site of today's Terminal 91), a steep bluff covered with a tangled growth of trees rose directly from the beach.

Of necessity, therefore, Seattle's commercial waterfront, beginning with Henry Yesler's lumber mill and wharf, was built out on piers over the water. Yesler's workers dumped fill off the wharf, extending dry, level ground out into the tide flats — the muddy area was left exposed at low tide but covered by up to 12 feet of water at high tide. Other landowners followed Yesler's example, using fill and pilings to create space on which to build docks, warehouses, and stores. In 1876, Front Street, the main business street running north from Yesler's Wharf, was graded and filled behind a wooden bulkhead above the beach, from which small docks stretched out into the bay. By the 1880s, new streets — Post Alley and Western Avenue — were being built beyond Front Street on fill and pilings over the tide flats.

ABOVE: Elevated railroad tracks approaching King Street coal docks, Seattle, ca. 1889.

OPPOSITE: Postcards provide early views of the Seattle waterfront.

TOP: Logs await shipment at King Street coal bunkers where vessels also refueled, 1889.

SECOND: A view of the Seattle waterfront, ca. 1907.

THIRD: Delivery wagons of the Seattle Coal and Fuel Company, Railroad Avenue S and Dearborn Street, ca. 1909.

BOTTOM: Activity along Railroad Avenue.

YESLER'S WHARF

The origins of Seattle — indeed, its very location — were based on the needs of maritime commerce. The founders of the new town were the Denny party: a couple dozen Midwestern immigrants led by Arthur Denny who had slogged their way across the Oregon Trail to Portland, and then caught Captain Robert C. Fay's schooner *Exact* up into Puget Sound — where they disembarked on November 13, 1851, at a spot along Elliott Bay that they would christen "New York, Oregon Territory." Amused by their grandiose dream, later arrivals soon humorously amended that to "New York, Alki" (a Chinook trading jargon term meaning "by-and-by" or "eventually"), and today that little dig is enshrined by West Seattle's Alki Point. Mere weeks after the Denny party's arrival, the brig *Leonesa* sailed in from San Francisco and its Captain Howard informed them that California had great need for logs to use as piles for building piers. The settlers got busy felling trees and selling them to Howard. And, with that initial transaction, the area's cargo-exporting industry commenced.

By early 1852, most of the settlers figured that their original settlement site was too exposed and blustery and they sought out a better one. Borrowing a canoe from the local *dxʷdəwʔábš* ("People of the Inside," or "Duwamish") natives, Denny and a few other men, using Mary Denny's 100-foot clothesline with a horseshoe as a sounding lead, set out to plumb the depths of the bay. Pleased to discover that the horseshoe never touched bottom — it was as deep as 200 feet just a few yards off the east bank of the bay — they climbed up the bank near a spot a few blocks south of today's Yesler Way, originally mapped as "Piner's Point" by the Wilkes Expedition in 1841. It was the site of a Duwamish village named *dᶻidᶻəlálič* ("Little Place Where One Crosses Over"), a trailhead from Elliott Bay to points east.

They returned on February 15th to stake claims and soon began constructing log cabins. In April the first group of the Denny party began moving over from New York, Alki. Initially they dubbed their new outpost "Duwamps," but by the summer of 1853 — and as their friendship with the main local chief, *siʔał* (1780-1866), deepened — the settlers renamed it with the anglicized version of his name: Seattle. In late 1852, Henry Yesler arrived and announced his intention to build a steam-powered sawmill somewhere on the sound. He was encouraged to stay with the gift of a strip of land (which became known as Mill Street — today's Yesler Way) that had direct waterfront access. That winter the construction of a wharf, mill, and cookhouse (from hand-squared logs) began and by March 1853 — the same month that Washington Territory was officially split off from Oregon Territory — Yesler's Mill, the village's first industry, was operational. The mill and its little wharf became the hub of the nascent town's economy, providing employment to both settlers and Native Americans.

When Thomas Mercer arrived in October 1853 with the town's first two horses and a wagon, he pioneered Seattle's first "intermodal" connections by carting goods to and from ships docked at the wharf.

By the late 1860s, the wharf had grown to a 200-foot length, and it expanded to an impressive 1,000 feet the following decade. Like much of pioneer Seattle, Yesler's old mill and wharf were destroyed in the Great Fire of 1889.

In 2022, Seattle Mayor Bruce Harrell and City Council President Debra Juarez, the first Native American person elected to the council, proposed naming part of Alaskan Way and Elliott Way "Dzidzilalich," in memory of the Little Place Where One Crosses Over. The new street signs between South Dearborn and Bell streets were unveiled April 24, 2023. "For us, it's not a renaming," Muckleshoot Tribal Council Vice Chairman Donny Stevenson said that day. "For thousands of years and hundreds of generations, this is the name by which we've called this place."

CENTER: Yesler's Wharf is stacked with lumber shipments while Mosquito Fleet vessels are moored at the adjacent dock.

ABOVE TOP: Old-growth trees like these gave truth to the legends of Northwest bounty and provided much of the region's early exports.

ABOVE: In the early 1900s, lumber mills dotted Puget Sound from Samish Bay to Olympia.

MAP: The Duwamish estuary and Seattle harbor as they existed in 1854, with circle indicating the Seattle settlement area and approximate location of Yesler's Wharf.

When railroad tracks reached Seattle in the 1870s, they too were built on piers and trestles extending well out into the water. This was due in part to physical necessity, but the many railroad trestles also reflected the history of Seattle's off-and-on courtship of and by transcontinental railroad lines. Seattle residents, like those of virtually every settlement in Washington Territory, hoped and expected that their home would become the terminus of a transcontinental railroad and therefore the commercial and population center of the region. But in 1873, the Northern Pacific, the first transcontinental line to reach the Northwest, spurned Seattle, choosing the upstart town of Tacoma, 30 miles south on Puget Sound, as its western terminus. Seattle leaders had offered the railroad 7,500 lots, 3,000 additional acres, and $250,000 in cash and bonds, but they could not compete with Tacoma's grant of its entire townsite on the west side of Commencement Bay, which gave the NP a nearly complete real estate monopoly around the new terminus.

Seattle was able to prosper despite this slight because its existing development, excellent harbor, and central position on Puget Sound made it the logical home port for the Mosquito Fleet of small steamships, and thus the center of regional commerce in lumber, coal, produce, manufactured goods, and other cargo. Still, Seattle civic leaders wanted a railroad and, with none in sight, decided to build their own. The local line never made it farther east than the coalfields of Renton and Newcastle, but it did set a precedent: Its tracks reached King Street from the south via a trestle across the tidelands, which at that time reached east all the way to the foot of Beacon Hill.

Several years later, the local owners sold their railroad to Henry Villard, who raised the city's hopes when he acquired control of the Northern Pacific in 1881 and promised to bring the transcontinental line to Seattle. In return, Villard requested a right-of-way along the central waterfront, which the city happily granted. Villard brought the promised branch line to Seattle, but when he lost control of the Northern Pacific in 1884, new management all but abandoned the Seattle link in favor of Tacoma.

In response, a new railroad effort was led by Judge Thomas Burke, a lawyer and real estate speculator who was one of Seattle's wealthiest and most influential citizens — and whose wishes were rarely refused by judges and other local elected officials. In 1885, Burke organized a local railroad with Daniel Gilman and other partners (the line's route along lakes Union and Washington is now the popular Burke-Gilman Trail).

It was Burke who conceived Railroad Avenue. In order to outflank the Northern Pacific, which controlled the existing right-of-way along the waterfront, Burke prevailed on a sympathetic city council to dedicate a new 120-foot-wide "street" (it would later expand) over the tidewater beyond the existing waterfront, and grant his line a 30-foot right-of-way along this street. This action was legally questionable because, while Washington was a territory, the federal government held title to all tidelands. But there was ample precedent for private use of tidelands in the many docks and buildings constructed on pilings and the earlier railroad rights of way.

Railroad Avenue began taking physical shape in April 1887 when the first of 26,000 piles, cut in nearby forests, were driven into the Elliott Bay wetlands. The first trestle, then just one track wide, was finished later that year. In 1889, Seattle's Great Fire destroyed part of this original Railroad Avenue, although a bucket brigade saved some northern portions. Railroad Avenue was one of the first things rebuilt after the fire, and it was broadened and extended, as were Western Avenue and Post Alley lying between it and dry land.

In 1890, Burke's Railroad Avenue right-of-way fell into the hands of the Northern Pacific, but by then the company had curtailed its efforts to quash Seattle. Well on its way to becoming the leading metropolis of Puget Sound, Seattle was now being wooed by another transcontinental line, James J. Hill's Great Northern Railway. Hill, a visionary railroad mogul based in Minnesota, was pushing his line across the northernmost tier of the United States to Puget Sound, which he saw as a jumping-off point for trade with China, Japan, and other Asian countries.

Seattle's location, harbor, and commercial development made it a logical place for the Great Northern's terminus, and Hill had the good sense to engage the persuasive and influential Thomas Burke as his local agent. Having previously achieved the creation of

ABOVE LEFT: James Hill, center, controlled the Great Northern Railway and the Northern Pacific Railroad, which eventually merged and now are incorporated in the Burlington Northern Santa Fe Railway.

ABOVE RIGHT: Thomas Burke built his law career in Seattle. The Burke-Gilman trail and Burke Museum are named for him.

OPPOSITE ABOVE: The Great Seattle Fire of 1889 as seen from the waterfront. The fire burned the entire business district, four of the city's wharves, and its railroad terminals.

BELOW: Columbia & Puget Sound Railroad station and docks, ca. 1882.

Railroad Avenue, Burke had little difficulty persuading the city council — over the vociferous objections of the Northern Pacific — to give Hill and the Great Northern a 60-foot right-of-way down the middle of the wood-planked roadway.

The Great Northern reached Seattle in 1893, and by 1895 there were four transcontinental rail lines jostling for position on the waterfront. Seattle finally had its continental connections and a rapidly burgeoning international trade. Japan's Nippon Yusen Kaisha (NYK) shipping line contracted with the Great Northern in 1896 to begin regular steamship service between Seattle and Japan. Hill soon launched his own ocean liners, the *Minnesota* and the *Dakota*. Dubbed the "largest cargo carriers afloat," they carried passengers and goods from Smith Cove to China, Japan, and the Philippines.

Moreover, because the city already dominated trade with Alaska, it was to Seattle's harbor that the steamer *Portland* sailed in 1897 with the fabled "ton of gold" that ignited the Klondike Gold Rush. Seattle became the primary jumping-off point for the swarms of gold seekers hurrying to Alaska and Canada in search of instant wealth, boosting the city's economy and population to new highs. The gold rush put Seattle on the national map as the gateway to the Klondike and Yukon goldfields. It also pumped money into local businesses, as the hordes of would-be millionaires who were heading north and the few who had struck it rich and were heading home spent much of their money in the city. The influx of capital and the demand for services helped boost steel, lumber, and other industries in the region, spurred the growth of roads, water and sewer systems, and other infrastructure, and boosted shipbuilding and waterfront commerce. In the first few years of the 1900s, private rail and dock owners built new wharves and terminals along the waterfront at a rapid pace. But despite the economic benefits, this uncoordinated development did not improve, and in some cases exacerbated, the tangled and dangerous mess that Railroad Avenue and the central waterfront had become.

A BLOT ON THE CITY

Well before it had reached that stage, some voices were proposing a different vision for the waterfront. As early as 1890, prominent engineer and municipal planner Virgil G. Bogue argued that all harbors in the state should be publicly owned. Bogue, who would go on to draft grandiose development plans for Seattle and other Washington cities and ports, had spent his early career working for the railroads, but he did not hesitate to criticize how they were using Seattle's great natural harbor. In an 1895 proposal for coordinated waterfront development, Bogue described the existing condition of Railroad Avenue, separating downtown and the docks "with trains frequently passing, switching going on, and cars and trains standing on the various tracks," as "an exceptional state of affairs scarcely equaled elsewhere" and "a blot on the city and a menace to the lives of its people."

ABOVE TOP AND ABOVE: Passengers pack onto the vessel *Victoria*, ca. 1904-1910.

ABOVE RIGHT: Alaska Steamship Company brochure.

Vessels of Puget Sound's Mosquito Fleet take every foot of space at Colman Dock.

MOSQUITO FLEET

For decades after settlers began trickling into the Puget Sound region, the main mode of transportation between new port towns like Tumwater, Seattle, Tacoma, Port Townsend, and Bellingham was via watercraft. Without horse paths, wagon roads, or railroads those newcomers — like the indigenous inhabitants all around them — took to paddling dugout canoes to travel, and then began importing or building boats and ships. In 1852, Bob Moxlie's Olympia-based "canoe express" service began making regular U.S. mail deliveries to Seattle, and in 1853 regular ferry service around Puget Sound began at Henry Yesler's wharf with the Gove brothers' side-wheeler steamship *Fairy*.

By 1865, a swarm of independently operated small steamers, which due to their sheer numbers, buzzing engines, and maneuverability came to be called the Mosquito Fleet, greatly increased passenger service to the growing number of farming communities, logging camps, and mills on Puget Sound and up the Duwamish, Snohomish, Skagit, and other rivers, adding to the hustle and bustle on Seattle's waterfront. It was largely due to the efficiency of the Mosquito Fleet, whose routes radiated around the sound from Seattle, that the Northern Pacific Railroad's 1873 decision to locate its transcontinental terminus in Tacoma wasn't a death knell for Seattle. Indeed, future banker and then-steamship operator Joshua Green later recalled: "These small Puget Sound steamer lines kept our merchants in close daily touch with all of Puget Sound in the '80's and '90's."

The Mosquito Fleet played a significant role in Seattle commerce well into the twentieth century and figured prominently in the passage of the Port District Act and the early growth of the Port of Seattle. Legislators and voters from small towns around the sound supported the act, and eventually created port districts of their own, largely to supply better facilities for the Mosquito Fleet steamers that connected them to Seattle and the rest of the world. Even at the Port of Seattle, where the first commissioners prepared the harbor for an expansion of international trade, serving the local Mosquito Fleet was a high priority.

The primary objective of the Bell Street Terminal, one of the Port's first projects, was to provide adequate docking space for Mosquito Fleet steamers, which were then at the mercy of crowded, privately owned docks that favored the big shipping lines. An early Port publication noted the importance of the fleet to Seattle's commerce, stating "these 'mosquito boat' lines are equivalent to branch railway lines radiating from the Seattle waterfront," making Seattle the distribution point for goods bound to "the myriad towns and settlements among the outspread fingers of Puget Sound." On their return to Seattle, the boats carried fresh produce and other products to the Bell Street Terminal, with its ample new cold storage space and a viaduct over Railroad Avenue giving easy access to nearby Pike Place Market, "enabling producers of berries, eggs, vegetables, poultry and fish from neighboring islands and across-Sound points to reach Seattle buyers through the public market."

Throughout the Port's first two decades Mosquito Fleet shipping remained an important part of its operations. Not until the late 1920s and 1930s did automobiles and highways supplant the waterborne transportation system, with diesel auto ferries replacing passenger steamers on the few remaining water routes.

ABOVE: This view of Railroad Avenue looking north shows the treacherous path pedestrians crossed to reach the waterfront.

OPPOSITE ABOVE: Reginald Thomson
CENTER: George Cotterill
BELOW: Robert Bridges

Bogue was part of a national Progressive movement, particularly strong in Washington, that advocated public control of essential services. Reformers worked on many fronts, and there were long struggles for greater regulation of the railroads and for municipal ownership of water and electric utilities (Seattle would become one of the first cities in the country to create city water and electric departments). In Washington, with its many port cities and strong dependence on trade, the battle for public control of the waterfront was especially contentious.

Disposition of the tidelands, which the federal government turned over to the new state upon Washington's admission to the Union, was among the most controversial issues when the state constitution was drafted in 1889. The railroads, shipping companies, merchants, and others who had built up their businesses on the tidelands insisted that they should receive legal title to the land they occupied. But Eastern Washington farmers, whose ability to export crops was limited by the railroad stranglehold on tracks and docks, joined urban reformers in support of state ownership. In the end, the constitutional convention compromised. The new constitution declared the state owned the tidelands but authorized the Washington Legislature to lease that land to private interests. It also set up a commission empowered to establish public harbor areas for incorporated cities.

To the surprise of many, the first state Harbor Lines Commission, created in 1890 with a three-year term, heeded Bogue and others who believed the entire harbor should be public. It designated a large public harbor area for Seattle, encompassing all of Railroad Avenue and much of the Elliott Bay waterfront. On behalf of the railroads, Thomas Burke immediately initiated a string of lawsuits challenging the commission's decision. Although the courts ultimately rejected Burke's arguments, he achieved his goal: The litigation dragged on until after the commission's term expired, preventing implementation of its harbor plan. Several years later, a new commission drew harbor lines for Seattle that carefully left all the existing waterfront facilities in private hands.

Although the railroads had prevailed, efforts for public, or at least coordinated, harbor development continued. In 1895, working for the King County Board of Tideland Appraisers, Bogue presented the waterfront plan in which he denounced conditions on Railroad Avenue. Citing successful ports elsewhere (he named Venice, Glasgow, and New York), the engineer asserted that "the greatest commercial success has resulted where there has been, either in part or in whole, municipal or other public ownership and control of dock frontage." In his plan, Bogue proposed a single terminal company to control and coordinate waterfront facilities. Bogue won the agreement of some rail lines, but opposition from the Great Northern doomed the plan. Nevertheless, the contrast between the efficient new port envisioned by Bogue and the existing waterfront chaos helped convince more Seattle leaders that a public body was needed to modernize the waterfront.

The Panic of 1893, a nationwide depression and the first of a series of economic downturns to hit Washington in its first 20 years of statehood, boosted reform movements. Three years later, reformers briefly banded together in the short-lived Populist Party to capture the state legislature and the governor's mansion. The party fell apart before accomplishing much, but the state lands commissioner it elected, Robert Bridges, went on to play a critical role as one of the Port of Seattle's first commissioners.

After the Populist Party imploded, the reform banner was picked up by the Progressives, who operated mostly within the existing Republican and Democratic parties. Progressives tended to be educated urban professionals. Along with municipal ownership, they advocated an array of reforms, supporting labor rights, women's suffrage, and prohibition. In turn, both unions and women's suffrage organizations were strong backers of municipal ownership. Not surprisingly, the longshoremen who worked the docks were especially interested in promoting public control of waterfront areas, both to create more shipping and therefore jobs and to provide a counterweight to the strength of private employers.

In Seattle, civil engineers were among the leading Progressives. Along with Bogue, there were City Engineer Reginald H. Thomson, who built Seattle's Cedar River water and power systems and leveled various in-town hills in massive regrading projects, and George F. Cotterill, Thomson's one-time assistant who went on to draft legislation creating public ports and to serve four terms on the Seattle Port Commission.

The strong-willed and politically astute Thomson argued successfully against James J. Hill's proposal for a massive Great Northern terminal on the central waterfront. Thomson foresaw that it would interfere with creating new industrial land south of downtown on the tidelands near the mouth of the Duwamish River (land that ultimately would become a major part of the Port of Seattle) and eventually persuaded Hill to bring the Great Northern tracks under downtown in a tunnel. The tunnel (still used today) did not eliminate waterfront congestion but helped keep it from worsening.

Meanwhile, Thomson and Cotterill took another small step toward coordinating waterfront development in 1897, when they persuaded the railroads and other waterfront owners to accept a new alignment of the piers that projected out from Railroad Avenue. Until then, all piers were built at right angles to the street, but since the street, following the line of the bay, turned several times, docks on different sides of the harbor pointed at each other and, if built far enough out, would collide. The engineers proposed instead that all new piers be built on an east-west alignment. Along the central waterfront, where the shore and streets run southeast to northwest, this had the added advantage of allowing trains and ships to pull up to docks and slips without making sharp turns. The flurry of wharf-building that followed the 1897 Klondike Gold Rush, although otherwise uncoordinated, conformed to this new alignment, as has subsequent development.

Topping the hill on the right, the Denny Hotel (also known as the Washington Hotel) dominates this view of the Seattle waterfront and northern downtown. The hotel, located on 3rd Avenue between Stewart and Virginia, was razed in 1906.

INSET: This 1913 Port of Seattle map illustrates the advantage of a uniform east-west alignment of piers along Seattle's curving waterfront. (West is down in this map.)

Hiram M. Chittenden Locks on the Lake Washington Ship Canal.

HIRAM MARTIN CHITTENDEN

Hiram Martin Chittenden (1858-1917) was the first president of the Port of Seattle Commission. Chittenden spent most of his working life with the U.S. Army Corps of Engineers where he was involved in the early development of Yellowstone National Park and in navigation, irrigation, and flood-control projects on a number of the nation's inland waterways. In 1906, he became the corps' district engineer in Seattle where he played a key role in determining the final configuration of the Lake Washington Ship Canal and supervised myriad projects around the state. Chittenden served as Port president after his retirement from the army in 1910. His efforts to ensure the Port become a truly public entity did much to shape the future of his adopted city. He and his wife, Nettie Parker Chittenden (1856-1947), had three children, and all three were in attendance in 1956 when the Lake Washington Ship Canal locks at Salmon Bay – better known as the Ballard Locks – were named in his honor.

CREATING THE PORT

Cotterill combined engineering work with political activity. In 1907, as chairman of the state Senate Committee on Harbors and Harbor Lines, he drafted the first bill to authorize public ports in Washington, which would have created port districts with limited powers. In addition to those calling for public control of Seattle's harbor, the bill won support from many around the state who believed public port facilities could benefit their communities. These backers included farmers and merchants in small Puget Sound towns who wanted better docks to attract Mosquito Fleet service; longshoremen's locals from Seattle and Tacoma; and businessmen from Hoquiam and other port cities, who, like their Seattle counterparts, wanted to prepare for the expected trade boom when the Panama Canal opened. However, Governor Albert E. Mead vetoed the 1907 bill, and proposed legislation failed again in 1909, blocked by railroad interests and mill owners.

By the end of the decade, railroad obstruction of public harbor improvements in Seattle was driving even conservative business leaders and politicians, along with the city's two major newspapers, the *Seattle Post-Intelligencer* and *The Seattle Times* — all generally opposed to municipal ownership — to support the concept of a public port. Two long-anticipated canal projects, one local and one international, played central roles in the growing consensus that Seattle needed a public port authority.

Locally, almost from the time the city was founded, Seattleites dreamed of a canal connecting Elliott Bay to Lake Washington, the large freshwater lake on the city's eastern side, but disagreed on where to locate it. Some favored linking the existing waterways of Portage Bay, Lake Union, and Salmon Bay — the northern route on which the ship canal was finally built. Others promoted a southern route that was more direct but required cutting through the 375-foot-high ridge of Beacon Hill. The northern canal prevailed after General Hiram M. Chittenden, yet another dynamic and progressive civil engineer who would leave his mark on the city and Port of Seattle, took charge of the federal Army Corps of Engineers Seattle district office in 1906 and endorsed that route. Congress soon provided funding for the locks that would be necessary (and that were eventually named in honor of Chittenden), on the condition that local funds pay for the canal itself.

GEORGE F. COTTERILL

George F. Cotterill proposed Washington's first port district legislation, cowrote the Port District Act, and served 12 years as a Port of Seattle commissioner. Yet the Port was just one aspect of his long and varied career. A lifelong teetotaler and ardent prohibitionist, a civil engineer by training and a social engineer by temperament, and a perennial (but rarely successful) political candidate, he held many positions and championed a wide range of progressive reforms with varying degrees of success.

Cotterill was born in England in 1865 and moved with his family to New Jersey when he was 6. His parents pledged abstinence from alcohol and were deeply involved in the temperance movement. Cotterill inherited their zeal and for his entire life prohibition was his most passionate cause.

Graduating from high school as valedictorian at 15, Cotterill considered studying law at Yale, but instead went to work for a local civil engineer who taught him surveying and civil engineering. At 19, Cotterill moved to Seattle and did survey work for mines, railroads, and other projects. Eventually he went to work for surveyor and engineer for R. H. Thomson and when Thomson became Seattle city engineer Cotterill joined him as assistant city engineer. They collaborated on numerous projects, from building sewers and bicycle trails to filling tide flats and replatting the waterfront.

One of their most important achievements was developing the city's publicly owned Cedar River water system. Both men were staunch advocates of publicly controlled utilities, but Seattle lacked money to construct the Cedar River system. Cotterill seized on a novel funding scheme whereby the city would issue construction bonds to be repaid from the anticipated water revenues. The arrangement that allowed Seattle to build its public water system became a standard financing method for public utilities across the country.

Appalled by Seattle's "open city" policy that tolerated gambling, prostitution, and other vices, Cotterill ran unsuccessfully for mayor in 1900. For the next two decades he sought some office in almost every election, winning twice. He served one term in the state Senate (1907-1910) and one contentious term (1912-1914) as mayor of Seattle.

A Democrat in an era when Republicans dominated state politics, Cotterill frequently worked with like-minded Republicans under the Populist and Progressive banners. He achieved some of his greatest political success as a leader in the Progressive-dominated legislative sessions of 1907 and 1909. Along with the Port District Act (not finally enacted until after he lost his Senate seat), he helped win legislative approval for the state constitutional amendment, subsequently approved by voters, that granted women the right to vote.

During his tenure on the Port of Seattle Commission beginning in 1922, Cotterill went along with fellow commissioners George Lamping and W. S. Lincoln as they moved the formerly radical Port in the direction of the city's conservative establishment. He also pushed for tighter control of the waterfront to eliminate illegal liquor shipments — Mayor Edwin "Doc" Brown, no fan of Prohibition or prohibitionists, responded by presenting Cotterill with a corkscrew purportedly representing the public mood.

Cotterill was nearing 60 when he lost his commission seat. He eventually retired from a position in the King County assessor's office at age 84. Cotterill was 92 when he died in 1958.

In addition to building their own canal, Seattle civic leaders wanted to ready the harbor for the opening of the Panama Canal, which they (and their counterparts in cities up and down the West Coast) anticipated would bring large increases in waterborne trade with the eastern seaboard and Europe. Because the shorter water route through the canal would not increase train cargo (indeed, it meant competition for the transcontinental lines), the rail corporations that owned Seattle's waterfront had little incentive to prepare for more intercoastal shipping. Seattle leaders feared the city would fall behind rival western ports — Los Angeles, San Francisco, Portland — that were already investing in docks and wharves to attract the expected new shipping. Even nearby Tacoma, which had long lagged behind its neighbor in maritime trade, was catching up, and in 1910 began building Washington's first municipally owned dock. *The Seattle Times*, usually allergic to any whiff of municipal ownership, editorialized that Seattle should follow suit and "determine this question of city-owned docks in the affirmative." With railroads in control of the central waterfront, proponents of new facilities looked to the undeveloped land along the Duwamish River.

In 1909, the legislature, even as it rejected public port legislation, authorized King County voters to establish separate local improvement districts that could issue bonds and levy taxes to build the Lake Washington Ship Canal and develop the lower Duwamish into a waterway for large oceangoing ships. The King County commissioners approved a combined $1.75 million bond issue for the two projects, and two future port commissioners — Robert Bridges, the Populist firebrand, and Charles E. Remsberg, a Fremont banker, attorney, and real estate speculator — headed the campaign for the bond issue, which won easily in the November 1910 election.

Railroad attorneys immediately sued to invalidate the local improvement districts and managed to block work on the Duwamish Waterway for a time, but this latest attempt to obstruct projects that much of Seattle's commercial and business establishment considered essential was the last straw. When the 1911 legislative session opened, a broad consensus favored creating public port districts in Washington. Said Governor Marion E. Hay: "The people of this state are in favor of public docks and wharves and such harbor improvements as will aid commerce and navigation for the benefit of all."

The legislature passed the Port District Act, which Governor Hay signed into law on March 14, 1911. The act was drafted by Cotterill, Thomson, and Seattle Corporation Counsel Scott Calhoun, a young lawyer active in the Seattle Commercial Club, one of the civic organizations pushing for a public port. The Port District Act authorized the voters of any county in Washington to create a port district to acquire, construct, and operate waterways, docks, wharves, and other harbor improvements; rail and water transfer and terminal facilities; and ferry systems. The inclusion of ferry systems reflected frustration in King County and elsewhere with private ferry operators. A port district would be a governmental body, independent of any existing county, city, or other government, with the power to levy taxes and issue bonds, run by three elected commissioners serving

LAKE WASHINGTON FERRY SERVICE

On December 6, 1913, the auto ferry *Leschi* was launched from Rainier Beach on Lake Washington. Originally designed as a side-wheeler, *Leschi* was owned and authorized by the Seattle Port Commission, and was the first public, tax-supported water transportation in the Puget Sound region. The ferry was built in response to requests from Bellevue farmers who need a better way to transport their goods to market than by taking the passenger-only steamers then in service from Kirkland.

The Seattle Port Commission operated the ferry until 1918, after which the run was transferred to King County. In 1931, the side-wheeler was converted to diesel power and continued to operate on Lake Washington until 1950. The boat was then purchased by Washington State Ferries for use on Puget Sound. In 1968, it was sold for use as a salmon cannery in Alaska. Today, the Leschi's wrecked hull lies abandoned in Shotgun Cove, near Whittier, Alaska.

without compensation. Port districts were given additional broad powers, including authority to acquire property by eminent domain, to set wharf and dock rates, and to lease port-owned property to private operators.

Even before the Port District Act took effect on June 8, 1911, Calhoun and the Commercial Club organized an ad hoc committee, with representatives from the Seattle Chamber of Commerce, Municipal League, Rotary Club, Manufacturers' Association, and other groups, to form a port district in King County. As soon as the act was law, the committee quickly collected the signatures needed to place creation of the Port of Seattle on the county's September 5 ballot.

Recognizing that a public port would be of little use if the railroads and private dock owners dominated the Port Commission, Calhoun's committee also screened potential candidates for the three commissioner positions, endorsing three at a July 28 meeting. For the central district, the committee selected Hiram Chittenden, the well-respected former Army Corps of Engineers officer. The committee's choice for the south district was the combative former state Lands Commissioner Robert Bridges, controversial for his radical views but a tireless advocate for the Duwamish Waterway district. Charles Remsberg, the Republican banker from Fremont chosen for the north district, was supposed to balance the Populist Bridges on the ticket, but he was as committed to municipal ownership as his fellow nominees and in some respects proved as radical as Bridges.

With support from the press, civic organizations, politicians, and most of the business community, the proposition to create the Port of Seattle passed on September 5, 1911, by a wide margin, 13,771 votes to 4,538. Chittenden more than doubled his opponent's votes, while Bridges and Remsberg won by lesser but still substantial margins.

The Port of Seattle was a reality, but the broad-based support that led to its creation quickly evaporated, enveloping the new commissioners in controversy almost as soon as they took office.

Chapter 2: **BUILDING AN INSTITUTION**

Controversy arose soon after the newly elected port commissioners settled down to prepare a "comprehensive scheme of harbor improvement," as required by the Port District Act. Their plan included a large, deep-sea pier and terminal at Smith Cove, another large pier and slip on the East Waterway, a small public dock, wharf, and warehouse on the central waterfront, additional general moorage on Salmon Bay (the plan was soon modified to build Fishermen's Terminal at Salmon Bay), and new ferry service on Lake Washington.

Of necessity, these projects were planned on largely undeveloped land near the fringes of the developed waterfront. East Waterway, still in its infancy, was the portion of the dredged Duwamish channel lying between the mainland south of downtown and artificial Harbor Island. Smith Cove, site of the Great Northern terminal and piers, was north of downtown in the Interbay area between Queen Anne and Magnolia hills, while Salmon Bay marked the northern end of Interbay. Even the central waterfront terminal, which would serve the Mosquito Fleet and house the Port's headquarters for many years, was located at the foot of Bell Street, then well north of the core business district.

OPPOSITE: Fishermen's Terminal, 1913.

Harbor Island in 1912. Looking Across the Bay Toward the Business Section of Seattle.

Photo by Howell & Hagmeier, Seattle.

The new Plans for the development of Harbor Island and the East Waterway, Seattle, U. S. A.

But even as the commission prepared its plans, much of the downtown business establishment, headed by the Chamber of Commerce and vociferously represented by *The Seattle Times* and the *Seattle Post-Intelligencer*, promoted a very different view of the Port's proper role. Predictably, the railroads and private dock owners viewed the proposed public docks as unwanted competition. The press and other downtown businesses, which as a last resort had supported a public port to overcome the railroad monopoly on the waterfront, abhorred the idea of a public body operating commercial facilities like docks and wharves. They argued that the purpose of a public port was to use the powers of taxation, bonding, and condemnation to acquire land and fund comprehensive port improvements that private owners would not or could not undertake, but then to turn construction and operation of those facilities over to private enterprise.

And the Chamber, *Times*, and *P-I* had in mind a particular plan which fit that description: erection of a "Bush Terminal on Harbor Island." The idea of replicating the huge New York City terminal, famous as the largest and most modern in the nation, on the recently created and still-undeveloped island at the mouth of the Duwamish, first appeared in a comprehensive plan for the City of Seattle proposed in 1911 by Virgil Bogue. In that ambitious and costly proposal, Bogue, who had earlier prepared the 1895 waterfront plan torpedoed by the Great Northern, called for an ornate new Civic Center in the Denny Regrade, many new boulevards and parks, and extensive harbor improvements, including seven enormous piers and terminals on Harbor Island modeled on New York's Bush Terminals.

The press and downtown businesses strongly opposed most of Bogue's plan (contributing to its overwhelming defeat at the polls), but embraced the idea that a massive "Bush Terminal" type of complex would prepare Seattle for the trade that they expected to flow from the opening of the Panama Canal in 1914. Largely unstated but equally important to much of the business community was that if the Port confined itself to the Harbor Island plan, it would not own and operate other docks in competition with private enterprise.

That the Bush Terminal Company itself had little or no interest in building on Harbor Island did not deter the Seattle businessmen supporting the proposal, who recruited R. F. Ayers, a Bush advertising executive. Ayers left his job to promote the plan. The coalition pushing the Harbor Island plan also had the active support of Scott Calhoun, though his involvement was questionable, since the young lawyer who had helped draft and lobby for passage of the Port District Act was now serving as the Port's chief legal counsel. Calhoun traveled to New York City and returned in January 1912 with a "gentlemen's agreement" committing the Port to provide $5 million in bond money for the Harbor Island terminals — in direct violation of instructions from Port Commission President Hiram Chittenden that he was not authorized to bind the Port.

All three commissioners considered the plan deeply flawed. Not only did it place the risk on the Port while giving the profit to the private investors, but it was also an "absolute extravagance," unnecessarily large enough to accommodate not just all

Seattle's existing trade but all that from Puget Sound, Portland, Grays Harbor, Victoria, and Vancouver, B.C., as well. Moreover, as Chittenden explained, beginning the Port's development on Harbor Island did not make engineering sense. The island did not yet have any connections to shore ("Bush Terminal" supporters wanted the Port to build a tunnel or bridge), whereas the also-undeveloped East Waterway was immediately adjacent to downtown and would provide much better shipping connections. Chittenden wrote:

> It [the East Waterway development] will stay as long as Seattle lasts and its importance will grow with the growth of the city. As business develops it will expand down the waterway and along the Harbor Island front which, by that time we may hope, will have better connection with the mainland. In due time, the north shore of Harbor Island will come to its own, but to go there now is simply to force an unnatural growth.

Despite this explanation, which accurately forecast the Port's eventual development, Chittenden reluctantly agreed to add $5 million for Harbor Island to the $3 million in bonds the commission was proposing for its other projects. But he wrote the proposition such that the money would go to Ayers' Pacific Terminal Company only if it posted a performance bond to guarantee its obligations. Remsberg followed Chittenden's lead, while Robert Bridges adamantly opposed the Harbor Island plan, leading to calls for his resignation.

On March 5, 1912, King County voters approved all eight port measures on the ballot. The Port's comprehensive plan won overwhelmingly, as did bond issues for work at Smith Cove, the East Waterway, Salmon Bay, and the central waterfront, and creation of a Lake Washington ferry. The Harbor Island bonds also passed, but by narrower margins.

ABOVE LEFT: The Port's Bell Street Pier Rooftop Park, which opened in 1915.

ABOVE RIGHT: The Bell Street Pier in 1915 incorporated a wharf, a marine terminal with warehouse, cold storage, and the original Port of Seattle headquarters.

OPPOSITE TOP: Workers stack bales of hemp from India in a warehouse, ca. 1926.

CENTER: Harbor Island as it appeared in a 1912 postcard.

BELOW: Postcard vision of proposed Harbor Island development, ca. 1912.

Parallel piers improved navigation for ships and reduced waterfront chaos. This is the view west down Yesler Way, ca. 1913.

Debate over the Harbor Island proposal continued for 15 months after the bonds were approved. In August, the Port entered a contract with the Pacific Terminal Company, but it was not carried out. Ayers and his allies never managed to raise the required $310,000 in performance bonds, and in April 1913 the commissioners terminated the contract. Then, on June 17, voters agreed to the Port's request to cancel the Harbor Island bonds and substitute a $3 million bond for East Waterway work instead. Although the press bitterly blamed the commission for the failure of the Harbor Island Terminal scheme, voters also soundly rejected a proposal backed by the Chamber of Commerce and the *P-I* (the *Times* remained neutral) to add two new commission members in an effort to undermine the power of the existing commissioners.

RADICAL GROWTH

As the Harbor Island controversy was playing out, the Port Commission proceeded with its own projects. Soon after the initial March 1912 vote, the commission began its first condemnation proceeding to acquire land at Smith Cove, where the Port would build the largest pier on the West Coast, a half-mile long and a city-block wide, for loading coal, lumber, and other bulk shipments. The court action was necessary because the Great Northern Railway, which owned the land, refused to sell.

The Port awarded its first construction contracts in November 1912, for work at Salmon Bay and on the East Waterway. On Salmon Bay, the commissioners planned a home for the large Puget Sound fishing fleet. At the time, the several hundred purse seiners, gillnetters, and other fishing vessels were scattered in anchorages around Puget Sound, with no central point for provisioning and repairs. The "snug harbor" on Salmon Bay (as it was dubbed in the Port's 1912 annual report) became Fishermen's Terminal, which for nearly a century has been home to the North Pacific fishing fleet and a major economic driver for the region.

It was at the future Fishermen's Terminal, on February 15, 1913, that the first construction in Port of Seattle history began, with workers driving the first piles for two 1,000-foot twin piers on Salmon Bay. Three other Port facilities also began taking shape in 1913. The Bell Street Pier was built that summer, and the first floor of the two-story wharf building was fully operational early in 1914. Even before that, 25 tons of Washington Chemical Works salsoda (sodium carbonate) was loaded from the Bell Street Pier onto a Victoria-bound vessel on October 28, 1913 — the first shipment to cross a Port of Seattle pier. The rest of the Bell Street facilities — the second floor of the wharf building and a separate large warehouse and cold storage building at the north end of the pier, which housed the Port offices on its top floor and featured a rooftop park and a viaduct connection to the Pike Place Market — were completed in 1915.

By late 1913, the first wharves and warehouses on the East Waterway pier also were in business, and the Port had built the wooden steamer *Leschi* for the Lake Washington

ABOVE: The steamship *Minnesota* is moored at the Great Northern Docks at Smith Cove in this postcard view.

BELOW LEFT: Fishermen's Terminal is dedicated, January 11, 1914.

RIGHT: The Port's ferry, *Leschi*, carried passengers and vehicles across Lake Washington before the advent of bridges.

SMITH COVE

In early 1853, Dr. Henry A. Smith arrived in the bustling village of Seattle. He'd crossed the Oregon Trail from Ohio, to Portland, Oregon Territory in late 1852, and then had come north to check out opportunities on Puget Sound. Having heard of a proposed transcontinental railroad survey to the area, he paddled a dugout canoe from Olympia to scout the shoreline for the most probable site for a railroad to locate. He found the ideal sheltered cove along Elliott Bay nearly four miles north of Yesler's sawmill — a place with two villages the Duwamish people called called *silagwádsid* ("Talking: Mouth at Edge of Water") and *tʔákəp* ("Aerial Net for Snaring Ducks"). It would serve for constructing docks, and the flatlands behind could be developed as the tidewater terminus for the transcontinental railroad. So, Smith staked a 160-acre Donation Land Claim at a spot that soon became known as Smith's Cove and his mother made a claim on the adjacent plat just northward (today's Interbay area). As other newcomers trickled in, a good number agreed that the cove was a natural place for Seattle's future development and they bought residential lots on the two hills (today's Magnolia and Queen Anne) that flanked it to the west and east.

As he waited for those critical trains to arrive — they were the missing component that would allow Seattle to fully realize itself as a major seaport — Smith stayed busy. He cleared away trees, built a cabin on the western hillside, farmed, built and operated an infirmary, was appointed official physician for the Tulalip Indian Reservation, married and raised seven children, joined the Territorial Legislature — and consistently lobbied for a railroad to connect Seattle with the rest of the nation.

Dr. Smith also recorded a speech by Chief Seattle, leader of the Duwamish and Suquamish Tribes. The speech, one the chief's most enduring legacies and given upon his first visit to the city in January 1854, made an eloquent and cautionary plea to Territorial Governor Isaac I. Stevens: "Let him [the white man] be just and kindly with my people, for the dead are not altogether powerless." Later versions of Smith's translation were adopted as manifestos of environmentalism and Native American rights.

Following creation of the Port of Seattle in 1911, among the new agency's first priorities would be a 20-acre site (purchased for $150,000) that would come to be known as "Smith Cove." In 1913 the cove became home to Pier A, which was quite different than any then existing in the harbor. Rather than being built upon wooden pilings, the $1 million pier was framed with timber bulkheads, then center-filled with soil and rock dredged up from the adjacent slips. At approximately 2,530 feet long by 310 feet wide, Pier A was notable as the largest pier of its type yet built, and it conveniently provided berthage on both sides. That achievement was topped in 1920 by the Port's Pier B (later Pier 41). It was 2,580 feet long, built for $2,811,000, connected to eight tracks of the Great Northern Railway, and featured two huge warehouses that could hold two million cases of canned salmon, plus gantry and locomotive cranes, gas tractors, storage for up to 1.6 million gallons of oil, and waiting rooms for passengers cruising to the Orient.

ABOVE TOP: An untitled painting of Smith Cove, ca. 1880s, by Emily Inez Denny.

ABOVE: Longshoremen load the vessel *Taiyu Maru* at Smith Cove, ca. 1916.

ABOVE: Tractors ease the work of loading cargo at Smith Cove, ca. 1916.

LEFT: Silk from Japan, a lucrative cargo, is unloaded for swift transport to New York by rail.

This area would see much more history unfold, including the 1934 labor incident known as the Battle of Smith Cove and the U.S. Navy's takeover of the facilities (renamed as Piers 90 and 91) as a naval supply base during World War II. Today, Smith Cove's Terminal 91 serves as homeport for Carnival Cruise Line, Celebrity Cruises, Holland America Line, Princess Cruises and Royal Caribbean, as well as for Seattle's factory trawler fleet for at-sea processing of seafood. Smith Cove at Pier 91 is also featured in some episodes of Deadliest Catch, the Discovery Channel's documentary reality TV series that began in 2005 and continues in 2024 with more than 300 episodes.

ferry route. The side-wheeler's maiden voyage, on December 27, 1913, marked two historic milestones: the *Leschi* was the first automobile ferry built in Western Washington, and the Port's ferry service was the first public, tax-supported water transportation in the Puget Sound region. (Although the Port pioneered public ferry service and briefly operated a few other routes, it transferred the ferries to King County before the end of the decade.) Also in December 1913, following discussions with farmers from Eastern Washington and Eastern Oregon, the commissioners initiated construction of a 500,000-bushel grain elevator on the East Waterway at Hanford Street to capture much of the grain trade that previously had followed the Columbia River to Portland.

From the start, Chittenden and Bridges made clear that the Port would set rates to promote trade, not to make a profit. Rather than charging "what the traffic will bear" like private enterprise, Chittenden explained, the Port would set wharf rates at "the lowest possible basis" on which port property could be maintained and the bonds paid off. Bridges concurred, saying, "we don't want dockage profit; we want low rates." Moreover, the commission began planning two public cold storage facilities, one for fruit and produce at the Bell Street Terminal, and one for fish on the East Waterway at Spokane Street. The former aided Eastern Washington farmers, making it easier for them to preserve and ship their produce. The latter was for local fishermen, providing lower rates than those offered by private cold storage facilities.

Led by Robert Bridges, the Populist former union organizer, the Port Commission also took a radically different approach to labor policy than did the private waterfront employers. The Port adopted the closed-shop rule — all longshore workers at Port facilities would be union members, and private employers who used Port facilities had to comply. Union workers loaded a Great Northern train for the first time in 1914, when members of International Longshoremen's Association (ILA) Local 38-12 moved 650,000 cases of canned salmon from ship to railcars across a Port dock. While Bridges remained on the commission, the Port's cooperation was reciprocated — during the bitter 1916 waterfront strike that shut down most shipping along the coast, the Port supported the union and Local 38-12 continued to work the Port's public docks.

These radical policies on rates and labor issues further angered the business establishment. Press criticism of the Port Commission continued unabated, and in 1915 the commission was among the targets of a new conservative-dominated legislature, which set out to undo as many progressive gains of the past years as it could. A bill was passed adding four new members to the commission (thus eliminating the authority of the current commissioners) and precluding the Port from issuing further bonds. Other new measures limited striking workers' ability to picket and rolled back the power of initiative and referendum. However, a coalition of progressive groups, including labor unions, the Municipal League, and the State Grange, united to force a referendum on seven of the new bills, preventing them from taking effect. Voters rejected all seven in 1916. By then, the Port's astounding commercial success had largely put an end to attacks on the commission.

Ironically, it was not the opening of the Panama Canal in August 1914, but another event that month — the outbreak of World War I in Europe — that actually led to explosive growth in Seattle's maritime trade. The canal itself brought relatively little trade until the end of the decade — first landslides, and then the war, kept it closed to most commercial traffic.

The war, on the other hand, by sharply reducing shipping on the Atlantic, produced a corresponding jump in Pacific trade. Vladivostok, Russia's largest port city on the Pacific Ocean, became a major destination, as Britain and France shipped supplies to Czarist Russia, their ally against Germany. The war also stimulated Japanese industrial development as the emerging Asian power provided large quantities of industrial goods for the Allied war effort.

Seattle captured the bulk of new shipping to both Russia and Japan, thanks in part to its geographic position — two days closer by ship than California ports — but mostly due to the Port's new facilities. With its large docks on the East Waterway and Smith Cove, Seattle could accommodate bigger ships and load them faster than San Francisco or other rival ports. The Smith Cove dock, which opened in April 1915, featured a large, train-track-mounted gantry crane that could do the work of 15 men and six horses, slashing loading time and cost so dramatically that shippers diverted bulk exports from ports up and down the coast to Smith Cove. The Port Commission's policy of cutting shipping rates, making Seattle the lowest-cost port on the coast, also contributed to its new dominance.

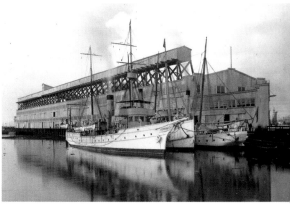

ABOVE TOP: Longshoremen load Samson Brand apples.

ABOVE: Schooners take on grain at Hanford Street Grain Terminal.

OPPOSITE: Gantry crane at Smith Cove, ca. 1916.

ROBERT BRIDGES

As one of the Port of Seattle's first commissioners (1911–1919), Robert Bridges brought to the table a hard-knuckled commitment to the progressive ideals of the Populist Era. Born in 1861 to a coal miner in Scotland, Bridges took to the mines at the tender age of 8 — and the brutal working conditions there encouraged him to lead a strike at age 9. His life-long commitment to seeking better conditions for the working class was thus deeply instilled.

Bridges and his bride emigrated to America in 1882, and five years later they had reached Black Diamond, Washington, where he found work in Pacific Coast Company coal mines. It was there that Bridges became a union organizer. In 1890 Bridges moved his family to Seattle where he opened a general store near the waterfront. With an angry political tide rising nationwide, Bridges fell in with the Populist Party, whose hearts he won after spurning a free travel ticket offered to politicians by the railroad. Instead, he *walked* from Seattle to the party convention across the mountains in the tiny ranching town of Ellensburg. Nominated for the position of state lands commissioner, Bridges was among the Populist candidates who swept the board in the 1896 election.

In 1900, the Bridges moved to Orillia (southwest of Renton) where they took up farming. He helped establish a drainage district in Orillia, and then focused on the underdeveloped lower Duwamish River area and for a time managed the Duwamish Waterway project. Then, when the concept of establishing the Port of Seattle arose, he declared as a candidate and on September 5, 1911, won the south district seat on its first commission. As Seattle historian Walt Crowley once noted, that election was "a high-water mark for the local Progressive movement, which advocated public control of essential facilities and utilities, and a pivotal defeat for the railroads that had long dominated Seattle's harbor thanks to imprudent municipal concessions." Taking on the presidency of the Port Commission in 1915, Bridges joined the ongoing battles with renewed vigor.

Bridges was dead-set on forcing plenty of change. When the Supreme Court ruled that year that the Port Commission had to stop selling ice to fishermen, he declared that such sales — essential for small-time fishermen competing against the big operations that had their own ice-making facilities — would continue. And, acting against the best advice of port counsel,

Bridges demanded that all Port of Seattle longshoremen join a union. A class warrior who distrusted the motives and means of war policymakers in Washington, D.C., in 1916 Bridges also spoke up against a military buildup and even forbade Port employees to participate in Seattle's "Preparedness Day" parade. Then after the U.S. entered World War I and the costs of food suddenly skyrocketed, Bridges arranged for the Port's warehouses to store at minimal cost the goods of hardworking area farmers so they could avoid underselling to middlemen in a panicked rush. But political tides were shifting once again.

As war fever took hold, political progressives and labor were attacked as disloyal radicals. In the March 1917 election, Bridges backed a ballot measure calling for the Port's passenger-ferry system to provide free service, and he simultaneously pushed for the creation of a public market in Seattle where struggling locals could shop for affordable foodstuffs. Voters rejected both propositions. In time, Bridges began to be outvoted on various Port policies and measures, and he finally resigned from the commission in August 1919. But Bridges wasn't done fighting: In 1920 he was nominated for governor by the new Farmer-Labor Party. As one writer (at *Olyblog*) put it: "He was establishment enough to be taken seriously, but dangerous enough to instill fear into the hearts of all conservative newspaper editorialists and give them hyperbolic fits. He was a radical with credentials." Still, Bridges lost — though he did capture 30 percent of the vote — and went on to become a representative for the Seattle Longshoremen's Co-Operative and maintained his farm until he passed away on December 2, 1921.

Historian Padraic Burke noted that, "When the Port was under almost continuous criticism in the early years of its existence Bridges was frequently the Port's most eloquent defender. He consistently took the Port's case to the people of King County, where he and the Port were almost invariably sustained. Despite his criticism of the Seattle business community, he was a brilliant businessman for the Port. He crisscrossed the country, again and again, persuasively arguing the Port's case before groups of small and large businessmen, and he probably brought more business to the Port than any other individual during the first years of the Port's existence."

ABOVE: The ship *Snoqualmie* is launched, August 1919. Shipbuilding was a major local industry at this time.

OPPOSITE: Robert Bridges, rear center, and his family.

The statistics tell the story. In the second quarter of 1915, Washington surpassed all of California in foreign trade, $45 million to $41 million (Oregon had only $3.7 million). In 1916, Seattle far outpaced San Francisco in shipments to Asia. In 1918, Seattle set a tonnage record for foreign trade that it did not surpass until 1965, and was the second-busiest port in the entire country, behind only New York.

In addition to trade, the war gave a huge boost to Seattle's shipbuilding industry, not previously a large part of the region's economy. From 1916 to 1918, the federal government spent heavily on cargo and war ships, and eight Seattle shipyards employed 30,000 men working around the clock. The Skinner & Eddy yard alone churned out 75 freighters, 8,000 tons each, in an average of just 54 days apiece.

CONSOLIDATION AND COMPETITION

When the war ended, so did the Port's era of radical policies and equally radical growth. Chittenden had resigned in 1915, some months after Bridges supplanted him as president, and Remsberg lost his bid for reelection in 1918. Finding himself frequently outvoted by his new colleagues, Bridges stepped down in 1919. Subsequent commissioners were much more aligned with the conservative establishment than the original three had been, and the newspapers and business interests that had vehemently opposed early Port projects soon generally supported the commission and its initiatives.

Under this new leadership — W. S. Lincoln, George B. Lamping, and George Cotterill (author of the original port district legislation) comprised the commission for

most of the 1920s — the Port abandoned many of the policies Bridges, Chittenden, and Remsberg had pursued earlier. It raised wharf rates to match those of private dock owners (though later in the decade it would face rate-cutting pressure from other public ports and even the railroads). Rather than developing and operating its own terminals, it encouraged local companies to lease Port land to build and run private terminals.

As soon as Lincoln replaced Bridges on the commission, he joined the Waterfront Employers Union (soon renamed the Waterfront Employers Association) and announced the Port would join private employers in hiring nonunion longshore workers. In response, Local 38-12 called a strike against the Port in May 1920. However, the ILA did not support the strike, and even the union local was divided. The strike failed disastrously. The Port became open shop like the rest of the waterfront, and there was little union activity until the bitter strikes of the Great Depression.

With the ILA moribund, the Waterfront Employers Association hired management consultant Frank Foisie to reform labor-management relations. Foisie created a joint representation plan whereby management and workers jointly operated hiring halls that selected dockworkers. Although this was essentially a company union (some workers derided the employer-dominated "fink halls"), working conditions in Seattle were better than at most other ports. Foisie's plan prohibited discrimination against ILA members (management elsewhere sought to rid the docks of union members), allowed workers to choose their representatives by secret ballot, and established a safety program.

One reason for the decline in union influence was the decrease in longshore jobs as Seattle's foreign trade fell from the record levels set during the war. For a few years, still-growing trade with Japan made up for the general international shipping decline that followed the end of World War I. In particular, nearly all the lucrative soybean oil trade from Japan passed through the Port's Smith Cove terminal — until Congress in 1921 imposed a high tariff that all but eliminated soy oil imports. In response, the Port initiated an aggressive marketing campaign in Japan and China, which helped reestablish Seattle as the leading port for raw silk imports. Great Northern's famous silk trains, which began serving Seattle in 1910, rushed the lucrative and fragile cargo from the Smith

THE SEATTLE WATERFRONT
PIERSON & CO. Photo
© 1917

Cove docks to the line's eastern terminus in Minnesota for onward shipment to New York City brokers, with 307 silk trains making the run between 1925 and 1932. Domestic trade and therefore total tonnage continued to grow through the 1920s, although at a slower pace than during the war years. The rise of highways, improvements in railroads, and use of oil pipelines all contributed to slow growth in maritime shipping.

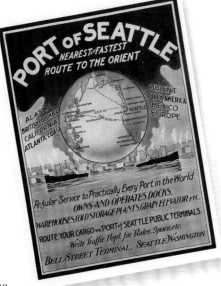

In addition, the Port of Seattle faced increasing competition from other U.S. ports, engendered in part by Seattle's remarkable success in the previous decade. Impressed by what Seattle's public port had achieved, many other cities in Washington and around the country established publicly run ports of their own, often drawing on former Port of Seattle employees to build and run competing facilities. A former Port of Seattle chief engineer helped Los Angeles undertake a major harbor upgrade. Many competing Northwest ports built large grain elevators and cold storage facilities, recapturing market share in those areas. The competition was not just from the West Coast — the ports of Galveston and Houston took over almost all the cotton exports that Seattle had dominated.

Ironically, given the Port of Seattle's early emphasis on cutting dock rates, newer public ports like Tacoma's (which was created in 1918 and began shipping operations in 1921) slashed fees to win business from Seattle. The resulting price wars pitted public ports against each other, to the benefit of private shippers. Moreover, railroad companies cut their dock rates far below cost, seeking to bankrupt public ports and force them out of business. In 1929, the Port Authorities Association finally succeeded in setting uniform wharf rates, ending rate wars between public ports.

By then, the Great Depression was looming, and the steady, if modest, trade growth of the 1920s would soon be a distant memory.

ABOVE TOP: Panorama of the Seattle waterfront, 1917.

ABOVE: Port of Seattle promotes its trade routes, Annual Report, 1928.

OPPOSITE ABOVE: Workers load raw silk bound for the East Coast.

BELOW: Silk trains met steamships at the Smith Cove docks to rush silk shipments onward to New York.

WILLIAM BOEING AND INNOVATION

Legend says it was the Fourth of July 1915 when William E. ("Bill") Boeing went to the shores of Lake Union hoping to finally get the chance to take his first airplane flight. Though the date of that first flight is debated, the thrill Boeing had that day is not. He was so taken by the experience that he waited in line again and again, sitting on the wing and holding on as the old Curtiss airplane skipped across the choppy water and into the sky.

Boeing, the Northwest's greatest aerospace innovator, had been fascinated with flight since 1910 when he and friends traveled to southern California to witness America's first International Air Meet. Though it took five years for him to experience his own flight as a passenger, the Meet was so exhilarating Boeing immediately took flying lessons in Los Angeles and later purchased his own plane.

With World War I raging in Europe, Boeing understood the need to be prepared and showed that to others by dropping cardboard "bombs" over a University of Washington football game, warning: "This harmless card in the hands of a hostile foe might have been a bomb dropped upon you. Aeroplanes are your defense!!!!"

On July 15, 1916, Boeing incorporated his airplane-building business as Pacific Aero Products Company. It became the Boeing Airplane Company the following year when he moved his aircraft assembly to the now-historically designated Red Barn in a former shipyard along the western shore of the Duwamish River, now the southern portion of the Port's Terminal 115. This move happened only weeks after America's entry into World War I and a U.S. Navy contract for 50 of Boeing's Model C trainer float planes. (The Red Barn was sold to the Port of Seattle in 1970 and was moved to the south end of Boeing Field in 1975 to serve as the original wing of the Museum of Flight, where it remains today.)

Boeing kept his company alive after World War I by building furniture and speedboats (popular on the Puget Sound during Prohibition), and with personal checks. Military and naval contracts tipped the scales toward survival beginning in 1921.

Boeing had delivered the first international airmail in North America in 1919. When Congress gave up on the Post Office flying mail six years later, it passed legislation to contract with private firms – making commercial aviation viable. Boeing entered the airline business by winning the federal air mail contract for the Chicago-San Francisco route in January 1927. The mail revenues of Boeing Air Transport (later folded into United Air Lines) underwrote passenger service and the development of navigational aids and airports. By 1928, Boeing Air Transport held 30 percent of air mail and air passenger markets in the United States.

The 1941 attack on Pearl Harbor sparked an unprecedented explosion in Washington's aviation industry and the Boeing Company built thousands of bombers, including the B-17 Flying Fortress and the B-29 Superfortress. (The Boeing B-47 Stratojet bomber first flew in 1947). The war years launched Boeing from a regional economic powerhouse to a major national business enterprise. Nearly 50,000 people worked for Boeing by 1944 and sales that year exceeded $600 million – 10 times the total sales for *all* of Seattle›s industry in 1939. Boeing's success in those years also contributed to Seattle's population boom. The Korean War, Cold War, and the Space Race only furthered the Boeing Company's footprint and economic growth.

"No living man has made the name of this city more widely known in the far corners of the earth than the original builder of Boeing aircraft," *The Seattle Times* wrote in 1956. "Boeing has become a household word in every civilized country of the globe and wherever its fame has spread, it has brought renown to the city where Boeing products first were fabricated." The free world owed him a great debt, the newspaper wrote.

Boeing retired from the aircraft business in the 1930s – though that wasn't the end of his business pursuits, which included real estate, Wall Street, and horse breeding and racing. For years, Boeing also personally cleared the annual debt of Children's Orthopedic Hospital in Seattle, which provided 90 percent of its hospital care for free during the Great Depression. The hospital would become one of the nation's top pediatric institutions.

When Bill Boeing died in 1956, three days shy of his 75th birthday, news reports talked of his indelible influence on the aircraft industry. Seattle Mayor Gordon Clinton said that, to many, Seattle had come to mean Boeing because of its tremendous effect on the airplane industry led by its founder's early vision. Today, the company has an annual revenue of more than $66 billion and more than 150,000 employees worldwide. Boeing was more than strictly airplanes: the company was a leading innovator in science, engineering and technology, and its name was, and is, associated with the innovative spirit of the Northwest.

"It's interesting how so many companies and ideas of huge national and international impact start in Seattle," said Rock and Roll Hall of Fame DJ Pat O'Day, who in the 1960s had captured more than 80 percent of the Northwest teen audience. "I give you not just Boeing, but Microsoft, and so many medical advances in the field of medicine and biomedicine, Starbucks, Costco, Seattle's Best Coffee, Amazon.com, Real Networks. The list just goes on and on and on."

Each day, hundreds of Boeing planes fly in and out of Seattle-Tacoma International Airport (SEA), and it too, has a long history of innovation. In 1976, the airport was the first in the U.S. to employ a full-time biologist and to develop an ecological approach to maintaining aviation safety and protecting wildlife, creating the model for other airports around the world. SEA Spot Saver, the virtual queuing program allowing travelers avoid long Transit Security Administration (TSA) screening lines, was piloted and refined at SEA starting in 2021. Today, millions use the program at airports across the country. That was one of many factors that earned SEA the travel industry's prestigious 4-Star Skytrax Airport Rating and designation as the Best Airport in North America in 2022.

Those advances and other Port developments are benefiting the Northwest's next major innovators – on the shores of Lake Union, in a Bellevue garage, like the one where Amazon was launched in 1994, or wherever they may be.

"Innovation is important to any organization," SEA Managing Director Lance Lyttle said. "It's more than just a values statement posted on a wall. The mechanisms have to be in place to make sure innovation is part of an organization's culture."

OPPOSITE: William E. Boeing

ABOVE: Boeing's Plant 1 (Red Barn) at the entrance to the Duwamish. River, where the Port's Terminal 115 resides today.

BELOW: The B&W, completed in 1916, was Boeing's first product.

27482
-CFM-

Chapter 3: **BOOM AND BUST**

The Port of Seattle had worked hard throughout the decade of the Roaring '20s to streamline its operations, refine its business model, consistently reduce its tax levy, mount an aggressive advertising campaign, and maximize the best usages of what had developed into some of the finest port facilities on the Pacific Coast. Still, serious challenges lay ahead. When the devastating financial news broke on "Black Tuesday," October 29, 1929 — the New York Stock Exchange had crashed — few could have foreseen that this event portended the beginnings of a decade-long global economic decline. The fallout would soon include profound unemployment, slashed governmental spending, and even wage reductions for the luckily employed. The only discernible upside to this bleak situation was that, primarily because of diligent planning and the regional diversity of Seattle's port, these negative effects were not quite as pronounced locally as they were for other seaport cities. But there was plenty of woe all around.

OPPOSITE: Fishermen unload their salmon catch, ca. 1920s.

THE GREAT DEPRESSION

The Pacific Northwest's economy had already been distressed before Black Tuesday arrived. Since prohibition had taken effect in Washington back in 1916 (with the adamant public cheerleading of soon-to-be Port Commissioner George Cotterill), many local breweries — including Seattle's iconic Rainier Brewery, which had long been the state's leading industrial employer — shut down, scaled back, or went into hibernation. Due to overfishing, the seafood industry was collapsing — the entire salmon catch of the 1920s was less than that taken in the record year of 1913. The timber industry also stagnated: Due to overproduction, local lumber mills — including those of Simpson, Weyerhaeuser, and Long-Bell — agreed to voluntarily cut hours or whole shifts to keep their crews working.

And things were about to get even worse. Economic hardships created a tense atmosphere all across America, fueling street gatherings of the disenchanted, some of whom became rabble-rousers crying for violent political revolution. Home foreclosures skyrocketed, and the ranks of the homeless increased with every day. Seattle's cheapest hotels and flophouses were maxed out, as the town became awash with desperate men and women who shuffled around town vainly seeking work. By late 1931, droves of homeless men began to squat on a large vacant patch of storied property owned by the Port of Seattle.

ABOVE: By 1937, nine billion board feet of lumber was produced and shipped from the Northwest annually.

RIGHT: Workers put labels on canned salmon, another of Washington's lucrative exports.

OPPOSITE CENTER: Hooverville, at the current location of Terminal 46, 1930s.

LEFT AND RIGHT: Hooverville just prior to final demolition, 1941.

BELOW: Hooverville's citizens elected a mayor and received mail.

HOOVERVILLE

A 206

A 207

As the Great Depression ground on, shantytowns began to arise in the hardest hit areas of America. In Seattle, they emerged along the banks of the Duwamish River, at "Louisville" on Harbor Island, and just behind Smith Cove (today's Interbay). But the largest and most infamous shack town grew on nine acres just south of Dearborn Street between Elliott Bay and Railroad Avenue (today the site of the Port's extremely productive Terminal 46 just west of Lumen Field sports stadium). Like many shanty towns built by homeless people during this time, it became known sarcastically as "Hooverville" in reference to U.S. President Herbert Hoover.

Originally the Hooverville acreage had been a mucky tide flat until reclaimed, in part, with sawdust and scrap fill from Henry Yesler's nearby lumber mill. Then in 1882 Robert Moran and his brothers founded a ship-repair business at the end of Yesler's Wharf. Both the shipyard and the wharf burned during the Great Fire of 1889, but within 10 days the Moran Brothers Shipyard was back up and running several blocks southward. This site later hosted the bustling Skinner & Eddy Shipyard's Plant 2 which produced many important ships during the boom times of World War I — and it was one of the initial flashpoint sites of the 1919 General Strike. But as the Depression deepened, Seattle's low-rent hotels, flophouses, and Skid Road missions filled beyond capacity, and in October 1931 the spillover of men began to build hovels in an area that held much history.

At one point, Washington Emergency Relief Administration investigator Donald Francis Roy reported that the site — which had become home to 1,000 inhabitants in 600 hundred shacks — featured "a conglomerate of grotesque dwellings, a Christmas-mix assortment of American junk that stuck together in congested disarray like sea-soaked jetsam spewed on the beach."

Twice over a period of months, the Seattle Police were sent in to evacuate everyone and torch

the village. Each time it soon rose again amidst the ashes and ruins. In June 1932 the distressed human inhabitants at Hooverville faced a committee of city officials who announced that the settlement would be tolerated — if a few rules were followed regarding proper sanitation, prohibiting alcohol, and not allowing women or children in. In addition, the inhabitants would be required to get out of their "gopher holes" and build true shacks. As unemployed logger Jesse Jackson (who was known as the "Mayor of Hooverville") recalled: "By this time the business houses had become more friendly to us and were very liberal with scrap lumber and tin, and the building of shanties got underway on a big scale. It seemed but a few short weeks until more than a hundred shacks were under course of construction."

A few years later, as WWII loomed and shipbuilding resumed, many Hooverville residents found jobs and the settlement began to fade away. The remaining men were evicted by the City in the spring of 1941 and on April 10, the abandoned Hooverville was finally bulldozed, and torched one last time. Two decades hence, the Port of Seattle made a farsighted commitment to redevelop the site into a vast loading apron that is now the site of the modern container-handling Terminal 46.

Ironically, eight decades after Hooverville's beginnings, economic hard times was one factor that let to a revival of homeless tent camps on various sites, including in 2009 at a public shoreline park at the Port's Terminal 107. Demanding more public housing, the homeless and their advocates this time mockingly dubbed their settlement "Nickelsville" for Seattle Mayor Greg Nickels. Although sympathetic to their plight, the Port announced that habitation on that land was illegal and that the tent town would have to relocate. Since 2017, part of the site has been home to the Interbay Village, 76 tiny homes. The Village is run by the Low Income Housing Institute and supported by a coalition of Magnolia and Queen Anne neighborhood churches.

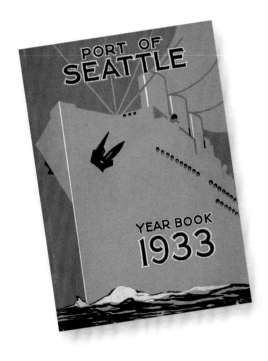

ABOVE: Port of Seattle Annual Report cover, 1933.

RIGHT: Washington State apples await shipment at Port warehouse, ca. 1920s. The Northwest had become the nation's largest producer of apples by 1937.

OPPOSITE TOP: Port Auditor Matt Gormley during his days in the Second Infantry.

BELOW: Railroad Avenue during seawall construction, 1934.

STREAMLINING AND SILK SALES

As the Depression deepened, Seattle politicians took to campaigning on the theme of streamlining the business of government, and the easiest target for such action was the salaries of public employees. Under such pressures, the Port tried to ensure that its 150 employees had some money coming in during the hard times. It announced pay cuts of up to 25 percent and instituted new measures, including cutting work hours, intended to decrease expenditures and increase productivity.

In 1932, the U.S. Congress passed the Smoot-Hawley Tariff Act in a misguided attempt to stabilize falling farm prices. The act ignited a backlash by various nations, whose in-kind retaliatory measures caused the international values of American goods to plummet. The Port of Seattle's core exports — apples, wheat, and salmon — dwindled to the extent that the elaborate cold storage facilities stood empty and unused. One of Seattle's most lucrative trades, Asian silk, dropped by 90 percent within five years. Still, other West Coast ports that were more heavily dependent on lumber exports, Tacoma and Portland among them, suffered even more.

But that fact gave no comfort to the Port, which just couldn't make up for drastically declining revenues. In each of these troubling years' annual reports, the commissioners attempted to strike notes of credible hope for the future, but by 1934 — five years into the Depression — they laid bare their souls, confessing that: "In 1932 we prayed for something to happen. In 1933 we just prayed." Still, the commissioners never wavered in their efforts. One initiative they launched to retain the domestic and foreign markets was an advertising outreach campaign in the huge Chicago and Asian markets. Locally, they won points in labor circles by maintaining full union pay scales for all longshoremen and stevedores — something the Waterfront Employers Association couldn't claim.

A NEW PORT COMMISSION

Yet for all the commissioners' efforts, an increasingly disgruntled public voted the entire Port Commission out of office between the years of 1932 and 1934, sweeping in a new crew who each ran on a platform of economizing Port operations. The complexities of administering the Port, however, ultimately led the new commissioners to govern with an approach similar to that of their predecessors — with the notable policy variation of opting to lease more Port properties to private businesses.

But the new administration's equilibrium was soon upset when a scandalous incident rocked the city. On Monday, May 8, 1934, the Port announced it had discovered a financial disparity in its accounting books. The following day, the *Post-Intelligencer* ran blaring headlines: "$70,000 Port Fund Shortage Bared; Auditor Gormley's Arrest Ordered." Matt Gormley — the Port's auditor — had reportedly been confronted at Port headquarters that morning and had then driven away, after saying he needed time to think and would return shortly. But when the citizenry opened their morning newspapers on May 10, they learned that Gormley — the brother-in-law of recently deposed but still serving Commissioner George Cotterill — had committed suicide in the Ravenna neighborhood. As the story played out over the following weeks, it seemed that Gormley had felt the weight of concealing various embezzlement schemes. Yet, it turned out that he personally had not stolen a cent. While the same could not be said of the Port's chief cashier (and his assistant), who may have made off with some of the missing money, Gormley instead had for 14 years been making occasional loans to Port employees to tide them over until their regular payday. These were well-intended loans that — with a little juggling of the books — were not necessarily paid back. But the clincher came when the investigation revealed that even Cotterill had given Gormley an IOU for a $190 loan — an IOU that became a political weapon for incoming Port Commission President J. A. Earley when it was discovered in a safe. Although there was no evidence that Cotterill had participated in a crime, Earley's grandstanding

ABOVE: Police officers in position during the Battle of Smith Cove, 1934.

OPPOSITE: Strikers block a train during the Battle of Smith Cove, 1934.

succeeded in clouding the reputation of his otherwise highly regarded predecessor. As historian Padraic Burke wryly noted: "The only positive feature (and quite a small one at that) to come out of the entire Gormley affair was a resolution that the Port Commission adopted … to begin paying Port employees twice a month, instead of only once a month."

THE GREAT STRIKE OF 1934

Sharing the headlines in local newspapers that same May was a far more troubling story about ongoing and unprecedented maritime labor unrest, which came to involve the Port, transfix the whole city, and indeed, wrack the seaport towns of the entire West Coast. From May 9 to July 31, Seattle's harbor was paralyzed by a strike that poisoned labor-management relations for the following decade and a half. The struggle pitted the International Longshoremen's Association (ILA) against steamship owners, police, and hostile public officials, and it would prove to be one of the most significant and bitter clashes of the century.

The trouble was sparked when the Waterfront Employers Association (WEA) refused to negotiate with the ILA — triggering a strike down the entire coast. Led by Harry Bridges — a spirited Australian sailor and dockworker who had emigrated to America in 1920 and would remain active in union leadership for four decades — the workers struck to demand a coastwide contract with wage and hour improvements and an end to practices such as "the speed-up" (when workers were driven to work harder without commensurate pay) and "the shape-up" (when employers handpicked who would work each day). A key demand was the establishment of hiring halls run by unions, not bosses. In Seattle, members of ILA Local 38-12 and allied maritime unions concentrated on stopping trains serving the waterfront and blocking the use of strike-breaking "scabs" on the docks.

Initially, the longshoremen had broad union support, including that of the International Brotherhood of Teamsters, which represented the workers who drove the horse wagons (and later trucks) that hauled away the goods unloaded from ships by the longshoremen. At that time, the teamsters' leader was Belltown's nationally famous tough-guy, Dave Beck. Though a standup union man through and through, Beck always believed that a strike should be labor's last resort — so Local 38-12 was no doubt ecstatic when he told teamsters not to cross ILA picket lines. However, that elation evaporated two days later when Beck — under intense pressure from politicians in Washington, D.C. — reversed his position. But the teamsters rebelled and ignored Beck's order to cross the longshoremen's lines. Nevertheless, his decision to yield sparked decades of hostility between the two union groups.

During the impasse, various local lumber mills were shuttered — with four closing for good — and shipping companies threatened to relocate to less turbulent Los Angeles. By mid-June, a tentative settlement was offered to ILA members for ratification. As they debated the proposal, newly installed Seattle Mayor Charles L. Smith decreed a "state of emergency" on June 14 and mobilized police to "open" the port, leading to a standoff with

UNION LONGSHORE WORKERS IN SEATTLE

The workers who unload the giant cargo ships at Port of Seattle marine terminals — truck drivers on the docks, cargo handling equipment operators, the cargo handlers in the holds, and the elite operators who maneuver the giant container cranes from small cabs slung under the crane booms — are all members of Seattle Local 19 of the International Longshore and Warehouse Union (ILWU), the heir and embodiment of a long, proud history of Seattle longshore unions. The workers at the cruise terminals also belong to the ILWU.

Longshoremen were among the first workers in Washington to unionize, during the mid-1880s wave of organizing by the Knights of Labor and other activists. Longshore workers were motivated not just by low pay and the physical hardships and dangers of the job, but also by the insecurity of traditional hiring practices. Workers had to compete each day to be hired by stevedore bosses at early-morning "shape-ups," and favoritism and discrimination were rampant. During a March 1886 strike, Tacoma dockworkers organized the first longshore union on Puget Sound. Seattle longshoremen soon followed.

On June 12, 1886, three days into a strike demanding a pay raise to 40 cents an hour, striker Terry King gathered fellow workers in his small shack and they organized the Stevedores, Longshoremen, and Riggers Union (SLRU) of Seattle. Article 10 of the SLRU constitution set forth the fundamental principle of job control for which longshore workers would fight during the next half-century: in place of the hated shape-up, the union would dispatch men from its membership rolls, in strict alphabetical order, to work the ships. The strike ended late in June with most shipping companies on the Seattle waterfront accepting, at least temporarily, both union job control and the 40 cents an hour pay rate.

The early union gains were wiped out by the tough economic times of the 1890s. The SLRU essentially disappeared after losing an 1894 strike against a pay cut. In 1900, Seattle longshore workers affiliated with the International Longshoremen's Association (ILA), which had been formed in the 1890s by workers at ports on the Great Lakes. In 1909 West Coast longshore workers formed ILA District 38 as an autonomous branch of the ILA. The Seattle local became ILA Local 38-12, which would carry the union banner on Seattle docks through the great maritime strike of 1934.

Despite the years of organizing, however, longshore workers had made few permanent gains. Wages in 1915 were about the same as they had been in 1889 and bosses again controlled most hiring. In 1916, the ILA organized the first coastwide strike in West Coast history in an effort to win higher pay and more importantly a closed shop — an agreement allowing the hiring only of union members. Although the Port of Seattle acceded (and Local 38-12 kept Port docks working), private employers refused and after 74 days on the picket lines, ILA members returned to work, their demands unmet.

World War I accomplished what the 1916 strike did not. With trade at record levels and workers scarce, employers raised pay, agreed to an eight-hour workday, and (again temporarily) accepted

the closed shop. But within a few years of the war's end, employers up and down the coast began rolling back the union advances. When the Port of Seattle followed suit, the unsuccessful 1920 strike in response fractured Local 38-12 and basically ended longshore union activity in Seattle for 14 years.

It was only with the union victory in the epic coastwide strike of 1934 that the long-desired goal of job control was permanently achieved. The arbitrated agreement that ended the strike established the union hiring hall that still exists today. Longshore workers start each day in the union local headquarters, where they peg in on one of several pegboards for different job classes, and are assigned out by a union dispatcher in the order they peg in, without regard to seniority or employer preferences.

In 1937, Harry Bridges, the Australian-born San Francisco longshore leader who played a lead role in the 1934 strike (he was no relation to early Port Commissioner Robert Bridges, although equally radical in his views), broke from the ILA and led most West Coast longshore locals into his newly formed International Longshoremen's and Warehousemen's Union. (When greater numbers of women began working on the docks, the ILWU modified its name to the current gender-neutral form.) Seattle's ILA Local 38-12 became ILWU Local 19.

Bridges headed the ILWU for the next four decades, building it into one of the most powerful unions in the nation's history and winning significant additional gains for dockworkers. Over fierce objections from some members, he negotiated the Mechanization and Modernization Agreement that paved the way for containerization and other innovations while ensuring that ILWU members would operate the new machinery.

The "M&M" agreement did not prevent job loss (ILWU membership dropped significantly over the years from its high of around 40,000) or end all labor conflicts — there were coastwide work stoppages in 1971 and 2002 — but it did usher in an era of significantly greater cooperation. Today, ILWU Local 19 functions much more as a partner with the Port and private companies in efforts to improve working conditions, boost production, and attract trade to Seattle.

In 2015, 29 West Coast shipping terminals, including Seattle, halted normal operations creating a backlog of goods waiting to move. The work stoppage was resolved after nine months of negotiations, including four days with U.S. Labor Secretary Tom Perez, who was sent to California by President Obama to help resolve the dispute.

CENTER: Longshoremen painstakingly load break-bulk cargo with cargo pallets and ship's gear — a vast difference from today's containers and 300-foot-high cranes.

CENTER INSET: An ILWU worker loads apples in a ship's hold at a Port container terminal, 1999.

TOP: ILWU members await job assignments at the hiring hall, 1981.

ABOVE: Yard activity at Terminal 18, 2023.

Strikers gather at the pier entrance during the Battle of Smith Cove, 1934.

pickets the following day. On June 16, all but the ILA's Los Angeles local rejected the terms of the draft settlement. Thus began the famous "Battle of Smith Cove."

THE BATTLE OF SMITH COVE

To prepare for expected conflict, the City of Seattle and King County had massed 300 city police, 200 "special deputies," and 60 state troopers, who were met at Piers 40-41 (now Terminal 91) by 600 unarmed pickets. Meanwhile, 18 ships waited offshore to land their cargo, while a squad of scabs huddled aboard an old steamer at the end of the dock. On June 21, strikers halted a Great Northern train en route to the piers, and mounted police charged with clubs and tear gas. The workers stood their ground and carried the day. But subsequent confrontations turned uglier, with violence escalating at every major West Coast port. Seattle saw ILA leader Shelvy Daffron killed and then King County Sheriff's Special Deputy Steve S. Watson disarmed by a crowd and shot with his own gun.

By this point, the economic effects of the strike were even starker: The ongoing labor unrest had brought waterfront commerce to a standstill. President Franklin Roosevelt and the National Longshoremen's Board (NLB) offered to arbitrate an end to the strike. On July 21, union members voted to accept their proposal, and strikers all along the coast went back to work on July 31. The arbitration decision, issued in October, granted wage increases to 95 cents an hour (the workers had wanted $1) for straight time and $1.50 for overtime, a shorter week of 30 hours, and a six-hour day. In addition, it established that the "hiring of all longshoremen shall be through halls maintained and operated jointly," but "the dispatcher shall be selected by the International Longshoremen's Association." This was a major victory. The ILA had won virtually all its demands, and the arbitration result firmly established the rights of waterfront workers nationwide.

LABOR STRIFE CONTINUES

But just a few years later, on January 5, 1938, 1,500 Seattle longshoremen struck again in a dispute over the interpretation of a year-old contract with the WEA. All movement of cargo across the Seattle waterfront ceased, and the Port of Seattle necessarily shut down. For a week, ships were diverted to Tacoma and other ports for unloading, until U.S.

Maritime Commission Chairman Joseph P. Kennedy (father of future U.S. President John F. Kennedy) stepped in and this latest dispute was submitted to the NLB for arbitration.

Such crises earned Seattle the reputation in business circles as the least cooperative port town on the coast, and its port would decline in the decades ahead. Indeed, the city as a whole stagnated during the Great Depression. Seattle's population had nearly tripled from 80,871 to 237,174 between 1900 and 1910; between 1910 and 1920, it grew to 315,685 (about 33 percent); but in the 1930s, it increased by fewer than 3,000 people. For all the desperate transience of the American populace during those terrible days, the mobile and migratory had little reason to come to Seattle.

THE WAR YEARS

The first rumblings of war in Europe in 1939 brought back frightful memories of World War I. Direct effects included the withdrawal of various foreign trade partners and shipping companies, as well as trade embargoes that caused a contraction of business activity at the Port. In particular, the shipment of scrap iron to Japan from Seattle — which had been one bright spot in the depressed economy of the 1930s — was instantly halted. Also stymied was another of the Port's key exports — Eastern Washington's famous apple crop, whose main overseas market had been Europe.

German submarine attacks on ships of all flags crossing the Atlantic Ocean had a twofold impact on business. The first was to severely reduce the shipping tonnage of American ports in general. The second was to spark a need for increased American shipping across the Pacific with Siberian Russia — a change that actually resulted in a sizable uptick in business based in Seattle. In addition, the Maritime Commission awarded Harbor Island–based Seattle-Tacoma Shipbuilding Corporation a $10.6 million contract to build five C-1 freighters. When the U.S. government launched a crash program to rearm the U.S. Navy and the merchant marine services with new ships, the same firm scored a huge contract to build 20 destroyers. This new maritime activity represented the beginning of a historic boom.

Additional governmental actions altered the Port's fortunes. In March 1941, the U.S. Navy initiated a takeover of the enormous Piers 40 and 41 at Smith Cove, which were recognized as the largest of their type in the world, and which remained the most massive in America for many years. Even though America had not yet joined the distant war, the regional economy was already humming. The unemployment rate had fallen to a point that Seattle's Hooverville had become an anachronism. Accordingly, in April 1941, port commissioners — now seeing a need for more space to conduct rapidly increasing maritime business — ordered that the shanty town be bulldozed to make way for a major new terminal.

Earlier that year, the Washington State Legislature, as part of efforts to ensure adequate wartime preparedness, enacted a law granting new powers to port districts — including one to issue without public approval revenue bonds to finance the construction

TOP: Sailors march across the Bell Street Pier viaduct, ca. 1930s. Bell Street Pier, today's Pier 66, was the original Port headquarters.

ABOVE: Hanford Street Grain Terminal, with a capacity of 1.5 million bushels, served as Seattle's main export site for Eastern Washington and Midwest grain from 1915 to 1970.

ABOVE: A family is reunited when a World War II ship returns to Seattle. During World War II and the Korean War, thousands of sailors and soldiers shipped out and came home through Seattle's Army Port of Embarkation, then located at Piers 36, 37, 38, and 39.

ABOVE RIGHT: Troops line up to board ship at the Port of Embarkation.

OPPOSITE TOP: Port of Seattle Commission President Horace Chapman, Port of Tacoma Commission President Fred Marvin, U.S. Representative (later Senator) Warren Magnuson, and Governor Arthur Langlie break ground on January 2, 1943, for the airport at Bow Lake, soon to be called Seattle-Tacoma International Airport.

BOTTOM: Port officials celebrate the first landing on the new runway at Sea-Tac, October 31, 1944.

of piers, wharves, terminals, warehouses, and other improvements for national defense. Although it raised concerns that the Port would now face less public scrutiny, the new authority enabled the Port to purchase Harbor Island's East Waterway Dock and to begin construction of the new $2.8 million Pier 42 (today included as part of Terminal 46). The project was notable for the sheer quantity of landfill required. The bay was so deep at this section that 60 feet of dredging spoils from adjacent slips was dumped in. Then hundreds of 40- to 70-foot pilings were driven in. Finally, the face of the bulkhead comprised 82- to 120-foot creosote-treated timbers. Upon that substructure, the Port built two 1,000-foot-long sheds and many modern facilities that were unprecedented on Seattle's waterfront. In addition, the Port built a $335,000 grain elevator at the Hanford Street facility.

In July 1941, Franklin Delano Roosevelt signed a presidential order halting trade with one of Seattle's biggest partners, Japan, whose warring aggression in Asia had become unacceptable. Then, after America entered the war following the December 7, 1941, Japanese attack on Pearl Harbor, Seattle's waterfront itself was radically transformed. The U.S. military effectively took control of the entire harbor to aid the war effort, imposing a new numbering system to help make better sense of the illogically named array of piers, wharves, and terminals that had sprouted over the previous nine decades. Most significantly, the piers at Smith Cove became Piers 90 and 91. On the central waterfront, the Port's Bell Street Pier officially became Pier 66. The Army rebuilt the Pacific Company Terminal as Pier 36 and built Piers 37, 38, and 39. Those four piers collectively became an official Port of Embarkation for the duration of the four-year war (today, that area comprises part of Terminal 46, with Pier 36 remaining the U.S. Coast Guard base).

Although the government's announcement in February 1942 placing all coastal ships in war service obliterated normal commercial activities in Seattle's harbor and elsewhere, the outbreak of war instantly fired up other sectors of the local wartime economy. The military needed aircraft, and Seattle's Boeing Airplane Company (now The Boeing Company) quickly ramped up to produce warplanes, including the mighty B-17 and B-29 bombers. Also, Seattle's shipyards and docks became a magnet for an influx of civilians to the Northwest, most arriving with the fervent hope of putting the Depression years behind them with new, well-paying jobs.

A NEW DUTY: BUILDING AN AIRPORT

Besides taking over most of the waterfront, the military was soon monopolizing the region's airports. Even before Pearl Harbor, increasing bomber production clogged Boeing Field, which, although named for the airplane manufacturer, was then King County's main commercial airport. The growing demands on Boeing Field, and the aviation hazards posed by the high ridge to its east, had already prompted calls for a new airport. The same 1941 legislative session that expanded public ports' ability to issue bonds also specifically authorized ports to build and operate airports. After the U.S. entered the war and the military took control of Boeing Field, McChord Field in Pierce County, and Paine Field in Snohomish County, the federal Civil Aeronautics Administration (CAA) offered $1 million to any local government that would undertake the task of building a new regional airport. The Port of Seattle promptly stepped forward.

Port Commission President Horace Chapman asserted that building the airport "is our duty, and if we can do it, we will." The commission voted in March 1942 to build the new field on 907 acres of forest and scrubland at Bow Lake, midway between Seattle and Tacoma. The choice of location and the name — Seattle-Tacoma Airport (quickly nicknamed Sea-Tac) — followed agreement by the City of Tacoma, the Port of Tacoma, and Pierce County to contribute $100,000 if the airport was located to serve, and was named for, Tacoma as well as Seattle. The CAA took charge of constructing the airport and its four runways (a primary north-south runway, a shorter east-west strip, and two crosswind runways forming an X), which were completed in 1944.

Despite a ceremonial first landing by a United Air Lines DC-3 on October 31, 1944, and inauguration of transcontinental passenger service by Northwest Airlines the following spring, Sea-Tac saw little commercial use until 1946. Instead, the Army Air Force used the new airport for transshipment of thousands of Boeing B-29 bombers.

AIRPORT LOCATION AND REGIONAL TRANSPORTATION DEVELOPMENT

When the Seattle Chamber of Commerce raised the idea of a major airport in January 1941 and started surveying possible sites in King County, the effort was helped by the Civil Aeronautics Administration's announcement that $1 million ($22 million in 2024 dollars) could be contributed.

Seattle wasn't the only city approached. The Civil Aeronautics Administration made similar offers to Tacoma and Vancouver, Washington, though their delayed decisions forfeited the grant money. With Boeing Field operating at a net loss—which it had during the first 14 years of operation—and the Sand Point Naval Station restricted from investing in municipal projects outside Seattle, all eyes turned to the Port. The Port held property valued at more than $30 million and an annual revenue around $2.5 million in 1941 dollars.

On March 2, 1942, at a Seattle Chamber of Commerce meeting, with more than 100 representatives from businesses, labor, and service and community clubs in attendance, the Port assured the crowd that it would take on the new airport project. The Port Commission followed through with a unanimous vote five days later.

Transportation was a key factor from the start. Of the two final sites—the present airport site just south of Seattle and an Eastside location where Bellevue's Lake Hills neighborhood is today—the then-rural Eastside site had clear advantages for saving construction time and money.

Area development would have been drastically different had the Eastside location near Lake Sammamish been picked. When Microsoft announced the move of its roughly 700 employees from Bellevue to Redmond in January 1985, one of the reasons given was the development opportunity that still remained. The area for the office park was described by one news report as truly greener pastures in "a forested 54-acre site." Microsoft's headquarters is roughly 3 miles north of the earlier proposed option for an airport site.

The current airport site between Seattle and Tacoma was picked primarily because of the advantage for passengers and transportation/infrastructure. United and Northwest airlines wanted the passenger flow from south Puget Sound and offered an annual $25,000 advance to get the current site completed. Pierce County, the City of Tacoma, and Port of Tacoma offered a combined $100,000 to pick that site because it was 20 miles closer to them compared to the potential Eastside site. That choice helped influence the airport's name.

The potential airport site south of Seattle also brought support from several of the area's newspaper editorial boards, too: the *Seattle Post-Intelligencer*, *The Seattle Times*, *The Daily Olympian*, *Chehalis Advocate*, and the *Tacoma News-Tribune*.

The area featured primarily woods, a riding academy, farms, and small buildings. Coyotes ended up on runways on more than one occasion in the 1940s, and the northwest corner of the field was home to a family of deer. Chosen primarily for its imagined potential, Port Commission President Horace P. Chapman said that from a commercial standpoint, practically every factor considered favored the site. It was, the *Post-Intelligencer* wrote, "the one and only short route terminus from this area for coast to coast, Alaska and Orient air service."

Seattle's mayor at the time, William F. Devin, predicted the space was destined to become one of the world's greats. Seattle Port Commission Vice President F. H. Savage agreed, "Seattle, if it goes ahead with the proper steps of development, is now ready to take an important place in world airborne commerce."

That quote from more than 80 years ago still holds up today.

The jet age that forced runway and terminal expansion in 1957 came a year after the Federal-Aid Highway Act, which provided 90 percent of the funding for the nationwide interstate network. The first portion of the Seattle freeway route received federal approval and funding in October 1957. The network would be completed through Seattle in February 1965 and statewide in May 1969.

The airport's redeveloped terminal was unveiled in July 1973 with 35 new passenger gates, an upper drive for arrivals, and a lower drive for departures. It was planned and developed in coordination with State Highway 518, the Burien extension to Interstate 405. The coordination allowed a direct link from the airport to Interstate 5, Interstate 90, and Interstate 405. State Highway 509, which was still being built when the new terminal opened, was planned to pass west of the airport.

In the decades that followed, some of the Port's contributions to major regional transportation projects came with ribbon cuttings and fanfare. Other projects were more functional. Each affected the daily operations of businesses in the Northwest whether the average person realized it or not.

OPPOSITE: The new tower is visible to the right in this 1940s image of early airport construction. The original 906-acre-purchase was home to a riding academy, farmland, some rural homes, and a rabbitry.

ABOVE: Originally called the Bow Lake Airport by the press, the site was approved by the Port of Seattle on March 30, 1942 and what is now SEA Airport had its formal dedication on July 9, 1949.

TOP RIGHT: Construction of the Ship Canal Bridge, part of Interstate 5 in Seattle, 1962. The first portion of the Seattle freeway route received federal approval and funding in October 1957, following the Federal-Aid Highway Act the year before.

BOTTOM RIGHT: Installation of the Satellite Transit System in 1972 was the first inter-terminal train system in the United States. Called the SEA Underground today, it is used by tens of thousands of people daily to move between gates.

Chapter 4: **INTO THE JET AGE**

The extreme wartime hustle and bustle along Seattle's waterfront gradually eased back to a calmer pace after the war ended with Japan's surrender on August 15, 1945. Although peace was welcomed by a war-weary nation, the transition back to a peacetime economy proved surprisingly tough, and the Port of Seattle faced daunting challenges.

Just five years prior, Seattle's Boeing Airplane Company had entered its booming years as part of President Franklin D. Roosevelt's "arsenal of democracy" by providing thousands of aircraft to the U.S. military — a task that allowed the firm to grow into the largest employer in the region. When the contracts for bombers were canceled at war's end, Boeing was forced to cut 70,000 employees. Another blow came when the expected postwar surge in imports and exports through the Port of Seattle failed to materialize. The stagnant business was partly due to the growth of the trucking industry and expanded rail services, but some critics also blamed passive Port leadership.

OPPOSITE: Seattle-Tacoma Airport is an impressive sight with its grand drives and art deco architecture, 1950s.

THE SHIPPING SLUMP

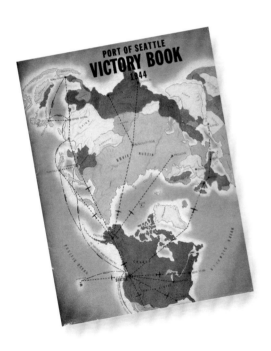

At war's end — and with the subsequent dismantling of various international trade embargoes and tariffs — it was hoped that a sense of normalcy would develop in commerce. But even as defense-related activity subsided, commerce through the Port failed to revive from the steady decline that had begun during the Depression. Though the national economy had expanded greatly since then, the Port's share of world trade, relative to the nation's other ports, was now less than 50 percent of what it had been just 15 years prior. In particular, Seattle saw its shipping business fall behind its longtime competitor Tacoma and other ports it had previously far outranked. Critical observers of the Port attributed the decline to uninspired leadership and questioned the usefulness of some projects. Another criticism regarded the Port's lack of an aggressive advertising and promotion program. As historian Padraic Burke noted: "While other U.S. ports [had] embarked on far-sighted programs to lure an increasing share of world trade to their harbors, most of the Port of Seattle's programs seemed to be ill-conceived and haphazardly executed."

The Port's commissioners — being fiscally conservative men, in general — were initially reluctant to launch expensive endeavors. However, some major changes to the central waterfront were driven by historical forces. When the U.S. military's use of various piers subsided at war's end, some reverted to commercial use, but such change was not always positive for the community or the Port. For example, in the immediate postwar years, Seattle's shipping industry naturally migrated to the Duwamish and Harbor Island facilities south of downtown, and soon the central waterfront fell into decline and disrepair. In fairness to Port leadership, the emergence of new transportation systems — not to mention the sudden availability of job-seeking military veterans — was bound to affect the general economy, including the maritime shipping industry.

POSTWAR LABOR STRIFE

The fact that Harry Bridges and his International Longshoremen's and Ware-housemen's Union (ILWU) had closed ranks with ship owners at the war's outset — an admirable alliance that focused on increasing productivity to aid the war effort — meant less to both sides as World War II wound down and the Cold War with the Soviet Union commenced. Bitter feelings — stemming all the way back to the 1934 Battle of Smith Cove — reemerged with a series of disputes that led to a coastwide 48-day strike beginning in October 1946.

In June 1947, the U.S. Congress passed the Taft-Hartley Act — a measure that tilted the power equation back from the unions to management. Hard-won gains that the unions had enjoyed since the 1930s were upset, and when contract renewal time came the following year, the WEA was emboldened enough to demand control of the hiring hall. On September 1, 1948, a 95-day strike began, a bitter action that halted all shipping on the Pacific Coast. One tactic the WEA used to break union members' resolve was to announce it would not negotiate with union leaders who refused to sign an affidavit declaring they were not communists. A long siege began with each side hoping to outlast the other. Then one company reconsidered: Seattle's Griffiths & Sprague Stevedoring Co. cut a special deal with the ILWU — granting a significant wage increase and tacitly acknowledging the union's control over the hiring hall. With the stalemate now partially breached, the Port of Seattle followed suit about two weeks later and likewise acceded to the union's demands.

Leaders of the WEA, however, remained adamant that they could not deal with Bridges, whom they condemned as a "communist." It seemed that an outside force would be required to break the jam — and that came in the wake of the upset election of President Harry Truman on November 6. Within days, the WEA, under pressure from some member companies that faced bankruptcy, sent in new negotiators, and on November 25, an agreement was hammered out that left the ILWU in its most powerful position ever. The severely weakened WEA desperately merged with the American Shipowners Association the following year in a move that produced the Pacific Maritime Association. The major downside for the victorious union was that the 1948 strike had fortified the reputation Seattle's waterfront had gained as a radicalized trouble spot. Business interests naturally began to consider expanding their use of the trucking industry instead. In response, union and management tried to repair some of this damage by publicly playing nice, but behind the scenes, the struggles continued.

ACQUISITION AND EXPANSION

In the postwar era, the Port of Seattle responded to newly emerging opportunities with the twin goals of stabilizing local employment levels and making its own activities and facilities increasingly efficient and modern. In 1946, the Port embarked on a $22 million,

ABOVE: Strikers hold signs reading "Our Union Today, Your Union Tomorrow" and "We are Ready to Work" at a terminal entrance, Seattle, 1947.

OPPOSITE TOP: Smith Cove docks, renumbered as Piers 90 and 91 by the U.S. military, in 1944.

BELOW: Special edition 1944 Port of Seattle *Victory Book.*

FISHERMEN'S TERMINAL

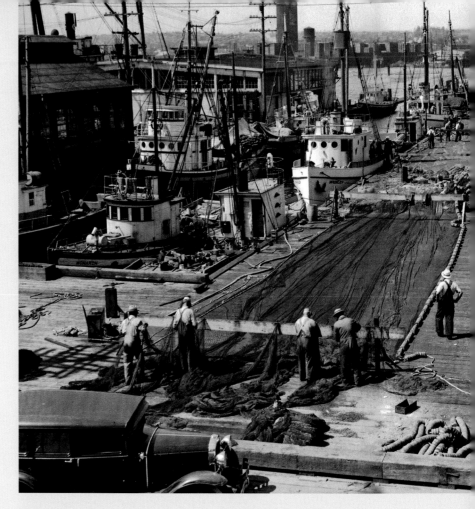

Fishermen's Terminal on Salmon Bay — the last major in-city wharf in America long dedicated to fishing boats — is one of the Port of Seattle's crown jewels. Salmon Bay itself — linked to freshwater Lake Union to the east and via a narrow creek (called "the outlet" by early settlers) to the saltwater of Puget Sound to the west — was a rich native fishing ground for centuries. Non-Indian settlers — like Edmund Carr, whose land claim south of the bay would ultimately be the site of Fishermen's Terminal — also depended on the waters of Salmon Bay and beyond. The newcomers included many Norwegian and other Scandinavian immigrants whose subsequent livelihood would help define their new home's image and economy: fishing. Because that community of fishermen largely settled in the bordering town, Ballard, they moored their vessels on the bay at privately owned marinas.

Soon after the Port was born in 1911, its first commissioners began to envision building a deep-sea cargo facility at Salmon Bay. But in 1913 an association of immigrant fishermen complained about getting gouged on mooring fees by private dock-owners. The Port was told that unless it provided them with a drydock facility, the entire industry would move to a different town. The Union Pacific Railroad stepped up and gifted the fishing fleet a strip of land (with the Port named as caretaker), area voters approved a public bond issue to finance construction, and on January 11, 1914, the Salmon Bay Terminal opened. Amid great fanfare Commissioner Hiram Chittenden gave a grand speech describing the new facility's mission: "To organize and solidify the scattered fishing industry of the Northwest, to provide a home for the extensive fishing fleet, to give such aid as the Port rightfully should give in protecting the fisherman in marketing his hard-earned products — this surely is an ambition worthy of the most earnest efforts of the Port Commission."

The terminal would eventually boast mooring floats, piers, docks, net lockers, and warehouses — along with boat-building and repair plants. In May of 1952, the Port completed a major, million-dollar expansion and modernization of what had long been redubbed Fishermen's Terminal — establishing it as the finest commercial fishing moorage facility in the country. Soon the bulk of the entire Alaska fishing fleet — which at that point consisted of 1,000 vessels — settled in, and Seattle began benefiting from the industry's multi-million-dollar annual contribution to the economy. Two new 625-foot piers had been built, as were two new net sheds; 25 acres for future expansion were added to the west; and a massive dredging operation improved the whole facility. The early 1950s also saw the rise of Byron and Helen Horton's venerable restaurant called The Wharf, which naturally featured a seafood-based menu along with a large live music dance lounge that drew crowds for decades. Waves of redevelopment upgrades began in the 1970s and today the terminal facility boasts 227,000 square feet of warehouse and light industry, office, and commercial retail space, including popular attractions like Chinooks Restaurant, the Highliner Pub, and the Wild Salmon Seafood Market.

In 1988 — the same year that the Port invested $13 million in improvements to Fishermen's Terminal — it became the home of the Seattle Fishermen's Memorial, a towering bronze and stone sculptural monument erected in honor of the more than 675 local men and women who have lost their lives pursuing commercial fishing since the beginning of the twentieth century. Yet that proud sense of maritime heritage also has sparked certain skirmishes. As the 1990s wound down — and the fishing fleet itself dwindled (the 371-slip facility had more than 100 vacant slips) — Port leadership began to believe that some economic diversification was necessary to sustain the terminal's economic viability.

In 2001 one controversy erupted after a consultant's report advised that the Port could raise additional revenues (required for an estimated $60 million terminal upgrade, admittedly needed due to deferred maintenance) by allowing some yachts and other pleasure-craft to moor there. Port leaders stressed the fishing industry's essential role in the local economy and the Port's commitment "to support the industry and meet the changing needs of the fleet." Nonetheless, a community watchdog group — the Friends of Fishermen's Terminal — alarmed about potential gentrification, unsuccessfully challenged the new moorage policy plans. Thus, today the piers are home to a mix of private boats and commercial ships — and Fishermen's Terminal remains a key fixture of both the past and present, one that has exuded a certain romantic aura for generations of Seattleites.

To prepare for future generations of commercial fishing and maritime industrial activity at the terminal, the Port is committing nearly $100 million in investments as part of a long-term strategic redevelopment plan to maintain docks for commercial fishers, enhance uplands facilities for tenants and visitors, and accent Fishermen's Terminal's history and legacy. These improvements include turning one of the Port's oldest buildings into the Maritime Innovation Center: a 15,000-square-foot facility featuring work, fabrication, and event space for new business incubators and accelerators, as well as anchor tenants.

decadelong expansion program that produced many major projects. Among the most notable were the $2 million acquisition (from the Pacific Coast Company) and modernization of Piers 43 and 45 to 49 just south of the central waterfront (all but Piers 48 and 49 later would be incorporated into the container mega-terminal at Terminal 46), the $1 million enlargement and upgrading of the Salmon Bay Fishermen's Terminal (which contributed $50 million in annual income to the local economy), and the $5 million modernization of the East Waterway Dock on Harbor Island.

But again, the Port's priorities were criticized. It was noted that such projects were mounted at a time when the Port's properties lacked adequate grain storage facilities, and the export market for that key commodity from Eastern Washington was thus rapidly shifting to Tacoma and Portland. The Port invested much time and capital into establishing a Foreign Trade Zone on Harbor Island that failed to generate the additional business activity touted by the agency's leadership. Such a zone would provide an area where businesses could repackage or relabel imported goods without incurring prohibitive duty fees, which instead would be levied at the final destination. Business interests supported the concept — one embraced by only a handful of other American ports — and after five years of intense lobbying by the Seattle Chamber of Commerce, the Port finally authorized the zone in May 1949. Then, on September 1, the Foreign Trade Zones Board granted the necessary charter. Existing facilities at the East Waterway were improved and Seattle's Foreign Trade Zone opened for business. What had not been adequately foreseen, however, was the amount of land required to operate a practical zone, and the additional customs agents and officers needed — an expense that would be shouldered by the Port. It was a no-win situation that soon saw the same business interests that had pushed for the zone demanding that the Port shutter it.

ABOVE: Salmon Bay was home to Hwelchteed, or Salmon Bay Charlie, and his wife Cheethluleetsa (Madeline). They owned 10 acres of land on the bay and supplied seafood to local residents on both sides of the channel.

BELOW: Fishermen's Terminal, 2004.

OPPOSITE LEFT: Postcard view of fishing boats moored at the public fishermen's dock, Salmon Bay, ca. 1914.

CENTER: Fishermen lay out nets for repair at Fishermen's Terminal, 1936.

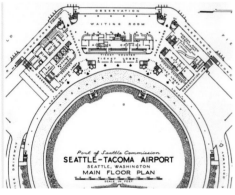

TOP: The first air traffic control tower goes up at Bow Lake (Sea-Tac Airport), 1944.

ABOVE: Architect's plans for the 1949 Seattle-Tacoma Airport terminal.

BUILDING FOR THE JET AGE

In contrast to the lagging seaport, Sea-Tac Airport began growing as soon as civilian use resumed, and did not stop. Almost continuous construction was needed to keep pace with demand, but the investments paid off, and the airport was one of the few financial bright spots for the Port during the 1950s. When commercial passengers returned in 1946, terminal facilities consisted of old barracks and a Quonset hut restaurant called "The Pantry," heated by a potbellied stove. Recognizing that such primitive accommodations would hardly meet the anticipated postwar surge in air travel, the commission placed a $3 million bond issue on the November 1946 ballot to fund a new terminal and administration building. The bonds won a sizable majority, but insufficient voters turned out to validate the election, forcing the Port to turn to its reserves for funding.

A dedication ceremony on July 9, 1949, celebrated both the completion of the new administration building and the official naming of what would henceforth be Seattle-Tacoma *International* Airport. The gleaming white building with its soaring control tower and airy, glass-walled passenger concourses was hailed as America's most advanced airport terminal. Regularly scheduled airline service at Sea-Tac had begun two years earlier in 1947, but it was only after the new terminal opened that Northwest, United, and Western airlines shifted the bulk of scheduled passenger service from Boeing Field to Sea-Tac. Almost immediately, rapidly rising traffic volumes strained runway capacity. In 1950, the Port commenced the first of several extensions of the primary north-south runway, lengthening it to 7,500 feet.

As the airport work proceeded, Boeing, which had already successfully produced jet-powered bombers, was beginning to explore development of a passenger jet. British and Russian manufacturers had produced jet airliners earlier, but it was the Boeing 707, first flown as the Dash-80 on July 15, 1954, that became the prototype for large jet airliners and soon revolutionized travel. Much larger and faster than propeller-driven planes, the jets also required longer runways, and the Port added first 80, and then another 170, acres to Sea-Tac and extended the main runway another 1,000 feet. With new lights and aircraft surveillance radar installed, Sea-Tac inaugurated regular jet airliner service on October 3, 1959, when a Pan Am 707 took off for Honolulu.

THE PORT IN THE 1950S

Meanwhile, the Port's lackluster advertising and promotion of Seattle's considerable harbor facilities attracted criticism once again. It was not until the 1950s that the Port even established a public relations department. When the Port did promote itself, it seemed to believe that it was adequate to simply point out — as it had during the prewar years — that Seattle was the closest American port to Asia. But a number of factors had by now made that boast less relevant. Chief among them was the decision by the U.S. Maritime Commission and the Interstate Commerce Commission to help offset Seattle's geographical advantages by instituting a new sliding scale of shipping rates that favored formerly disadvantaged ports.

Another blow came with the release of the Municipal League's 1950 report, which clearly documented a five-year decline in Port revenues since the war's end.

By 1952 — a year that saw a full 100 days of productivity lost to strikes in Seattle — business activity at most other ports had rebounded to levels not seen since prior to the Great Depression. Not so for Seattle, where the Port reported very slim profits.

That same year brought the election of two new port commissioners, Clarence H. Carlander and Gordon Rowe, but the infusion of new blood heralded not unity, but more division in the leadership. Not only did the new commissioners begin feuding with each other, they also began butting heads with Port General Manager Warren Lamport. In August 1953, the Port Commission abruptly announced that it was abolishing Lamport's position and that the commission would take over day-to-day administrative duties. Publicly aired charges of waste and incompetence flew back and forth between the warring parties; reputations suffered and the Port's business languished.

Weeks later, however, the Port hired the Seattle-based district manager of the American Hawaiian Steamship Company, Howard M. Burke, as its general manager. Despite the acrimonious atmosphere, he quickly focused on the challenges the Port faced. Burke saw that the Port needed a unified program of modernization and development to take it into the modern age. Among the projects he initiated during the 1950s were

continued on page 68

ABOVE LEFT: Ethiopian Emperor Haile Selassie addresses a crowd at Sea-Tac, 1954. From its beginning, Sea-Tac became a place to welcome dignitaries and celebrate events.

RIGHT: Postcard of the newly opened airport terminal.

ABOVE: Sea-Tac was all about elegance, offering the traveler fine dining, a barbershop, a gift shop, and even a lounge with jazz pianist and singer, 1950.

LEFT: The original main terminal offered a spacious waiting area, a view of the airfield, and comfortable couches and armchairs.

SEA-TAC ADMINISTRATION BUILDING 1949

Sea-Tac came into its own as a full-service international airport on July 9, 1949, with the dedication of its modern new Administration Building. The four-story, 234,000-square-foot office and terminal complex replaced the makeshift array of World War II-era buildings that had served Sea-Tac's first airline passengers. Planning for the Administration Building began as soon as Sea-Tac returned to civilian use in 1946, and construction was well underway by the time Northwest Airlines and Western Airlines inaugurated Sea-Tac's first regularly scheduled flights in the fall of 1947.

Colonel Earle S. Bigler, who managed Sea-Tac for the Port in 1947, supervised the project. Herman A. Moldenhour and Port of Seattle Chief Engineer George T. Treadwell designed the structure, and Lease and Leighland General Contractors built it. The Administration Building, which also housed the passenger terminals, contained offices for Port staff, the airlines, the Civil Aeronautics Administration, and customs and immigration officials. It included a weather bureau, the airport control tower, a post office, and waiting areas, concourses, an observation deck, gift and coffee shops, and other amenities for passengers. Eight airplanes at a time could load and unload at the building.

Ground traffic reached the Administration Building from Highway 99 (Pacific Highway) east of the airport, via an access road that ended in a circular drive in front of the building. The building was located just east of Sea-Tac's main north-south runway, and near the center of the X formed by the two crosswind runways. The two wings of the building, shaped like an inverted V, paralleled those two runways where they extended northeast and southeast across the main runway. Sea-Tac's initial runway configuration, with the crosswind runways angling across the main runway and a perpendicular east-west runway at the south end, was typical of military airfields of the time. Runways facing various directions were necessary because aircraft then were less capable of landing in crosswinds than those of later years (by the 1960s, the crosswind runways were no longer used).

The Administration Building cost about $4 million, bringing the total cost of Sea-Tac construction to $11 million by the time the airport was dedicated. The July 9, 1949, ceremony celebrated both the completion of the new building and the official dedication of Sea-Tac as Seattle-Tacoma International Airport. A crowd of more than 30,000 people turned out for the festivities. Port officials, the mayors of Seattle and Tacoma, and other

dignitaries spoke from a flag-draped balcony. In the main address, Washington Governor Arthur Langlie declared:

> Man, on Puget Sound can now tell the eagles, the hawks, and skylarks to move over and say "We, too, have at last won our place beside you in the firmament of heaven."

Any birds around probably did move over as military aircraft roared repeatedly above the Administration Building to salute the dedication. Newly developed jet fighters dazzled the crowd with their speed, while bombers, troop carriers, and patrol planes also passed overhead. On the ground, spectators waited in long lines for closer views of the newest military and commercial aircraft, which were displayed on the airport loading ramps.

Until the Administration Building was completed, most scheduled passenger flights had operated from Boeing Field. With the opening, the four airlines then serving Seattle and Tacoma — Northwest, United, Pan

American, and Western — shifted the bulk of their flights to Sea-Tac. Within five months of the dedication, the airport was serving 1,500 passengers per day on 60 scheduled flights.

Those figures were just the beginning. As the numbers of both flights and passengers increased dramatically over the years, the Port steadily expanded Sea-Tac's facilities. From the late 1950s through the mid-1960s, four concourses were added to the main building, increasing the number of airplane gate positions to 21. As the concourses extended north and south, and with newer airplanes better able to handle crosswinds, the crosswind and perpendicular runways were eliminated, while the north-south runway was repeatedly lengthened (two parallel runways were later added).

Eventually, in the words of Seattle historian Paul Dorpat, the ever-growing facilities "swallowed" the 1949 Administration Building. In 1973, the Port opened a new, greatly expanded terminal building, which was constructed over and around the original structure. By the end of 2005, a capital improvement program including a new concourse and central terminal yet again changed the look and space of the facility.

CLOCKWISE FROM TOP LEFT: The first airport terminal, 1947.

CENTER: Visitors by the thousands came to celebrate the dedication of the new terminal on July 9, 1949.

TOP RIGHT: Sea-Tac initially had four cross-wind runways designed for airplane landings and takeoffs in almost any wind direction. The jet age soon ushered in parallel runways.

CENTER RIGHT: A crowd of visitors tours a Northwest Airlines aircraft during the dedication of the terminal, July 9, 1949.

BOTTOM RIGHT: Northwest Airlines flight attendants pose during the dedication festivities.

CENTER INSET: Postcard view of the Sea-Tac Administration Building, 1949.

TOP: Surveyor at Shilshole, preparing for construction of the marina, 1957.

ABOVE: An early aerial photo of Shilshole Bay Marina, 1963. The marina was dedicated during the Century 21 Exposition, the 1962 Seattle's World Fair.

the construction of a $2.6 million grain elevator addition to the Hanford Street facility; the building of a 1,500-boat public saltwater facility along the western edge of the Ballard neighborhood — Shilshole Bay Marina (which boasted a public fishing pier, and in later decades a popular public promenade more than a mile long); the $850,000 purchase of the Ames Terminal on the west side of the West Waterway (now part of Terminal 5); the $600,000 purchase of Pier 28 (from the Chicago, Milwaukee, St. Paul & Pacific Railroad); and the subsequent $8 million development of a large, modern terminal between Piers 28 and 30.

While most of Burke's idea's were welcomed by area business interests — who happily noted that by 1956 the Port's foreign commerce shipping tonnage had finally recovered to pre-Depression levels — there was one major issue dividing them. In June 1957, the Port Commission unanimously committed itself to pursuing the decades-old dream of dredging a 550-foot-wide and four-mile-long channel up the Duwamish Waterway to provide additional space for industrial development. As the Port began buying parcels of land along the river that summer, lawsuits were filed by opponents who contended that the estimated $23 million cost for the project would ensure that it would remain unprofitable far into the future. While those suits caused a full year of delay, other problems also arose. In November, the tiny riverside town of Tukwila suddenly annexed 1,000 acres within the proposed development area, and the Washington Supreme Court ruled (*Hogue vs. Port of Seattle*) that the Port's actions in condemning land for the project was unconstitutional. The Port was forced to place the Duwamish channel project on the back burner.

CALLS FOR REFORM

By 1957, the Port owned 21 of the 88 piers and terminals on Seattle's waterfront. It was estimated that nearly half the town's annual income originated in harbor-related industries. Yet shipping declined throughout the 1950s. A particularly sore point for port commissioners was the rate differential certain other ports were granted to compensate for Seattle's geographic advantage. One particularly grating example involved export of Washington apples. The rate advantage granted by federal agencies to the Port of San Francisco allowed it to ship 78,000 boxes of the iconic Washington state fruit in 1954, while a mere 5,480 boxes crossed Seattle's docks.

In addition to coping with government interference, the Port had to deal with a series of reports finding serious fault with the Port during the decade. In 1956, the "Ocean-Borne Commerce of the State of Washington" report, conducted by the University of Washington's Bureau of Business Research for the Port, concluded that, in essence, the Port had failed to remain competitive with other ports. Then, in 1958, a League of Women Voters study documented that ports with governing structures similar to Seattle's typically lacked strong leadership. Compounding such negative analyses was yet another report — this one produced under contract with the Port by the consulting firm Booz, Allen & Hamilton — that reached unflattering conclusions. In addition to noting the obvious — that the commissioners had taken on too many administrative tasks, rather than focusing on their proper role of formulating policy — this study identified another core problem. As historian Padraic Burke wrote: Its "most damaging conclusion was that the Port was an aloof organization, with little contact with the community it served, and without a program of specific goals and objectives." In its recommendations, Booz Allen went on to suggest that the Port's first step should be to meet with a group of responsible community leaders and hash out a realistic set of goals that would benefit the wider community.

This spotlight on problems continued in 1959, when Seattle's NBC affiliate KING-TV aired a documentary, *Lost Cargo*, that chronicled the postwar decline of the Port of Seattle — a general perception supported by the Port's own annual report. Issued in February, it revealed that Seattle's shipping levels had decreased by 15 percent in a year that saw other West Coast ports reporting record gains. The Port clearly had some soul-searching to do. And in July, a newly elected commissioner, Thomas McManus, boldly demanded that all of his fellow commissioners resign — an idea area newspapers seconded on their editorial pages.

Against this backdrop, the election of November 1960 brought passage of two major measures intended to reform and update the Port. Voters approved a proposal, which enjoyed nearly unanimous political support, to expand the Port Commission from three members to five — including two elected at-large. Voters also passed a $10 million Port bond issue that would kick-start a new decade in which Seattle would move from last to first position among West Coast ports in shipping to points east.

TOP: Longshoremen load cargo with pallets and ship's gear, 1950s.

ABOVE: Port of Seattle Annual Report, 1957, showing trade routes.

Chapter 5: **REVOLUTION AND RECESSION**

As the Eisenhower Era gave way to President John F. Kennedy's "New Frontier," the Port of Seattle still faced — as did other ports — an era of uncertainty. And the Port, as a string of newspaper editorials pointedly noted, seemed stuck in the past. But this public prodding, combined with internal critiques, soon led to a remarkable turn-around. However, the change was not immediate. The 1960 election of an expanded Port Commission brought first a year of record-breaking maritime trade, followed by almost two years of decline, although this was partly due to personality conflicts on the commission.

POLITICS, PLANNING, AND PROGRESS

This floundering was duly noted by the Washington State Legislature. It held hearings in 1961 to explore the problems at the Port, which led to further reforms that ultimately gave the Port greater taxing authority and power to take the big steps necessary for making the agency more competitive and efficient. Other keys to the Port's subsequent success included implementation of nearly all recommendations of the 1958 Booz, Allen & Hamilton report. These included distancing commissioners from day-to-day operational issues, which

OPPOSITE: Miss Maritime of 1961, Julie Blonk of American Mail Line, showcases the Port's 50th anniversary. For several years, Miss Maritime rode the Port's float in the Maritime Week parades.

resulted in the creation of several departments: Planning and Research, Data Processing, Real Estate, Trade Development, and Public Relations, each staffed by highly regarded professionals.

These changes laid the groundwork for Seattle to be among the first ports to take full advantage of the coming revolution in shipping. For instance, the year 1961 saw the Port reestablish an office in America's heartland. That Chicago outpost was focused on increasing overland business via an emerging advance in the logistics of shipping: the move to containerized cargo. But before a clear path to a successful future could be established, one more breakthrough was needed: the adoption of an initial "Mechanization and Modernization Agreement" between labor and management along the waterfront.

MECHANIZATION AND MODERNIZATION

The emergence of new labor-saving machinery (termed "mechanization") and the application of new work rules requiring greater efficiency (termed "modernization") had been complicating labor-management relations along the waterfront for years. Both ideas had long been resisted by the ILWU, but eventually a Mechanization and Modernization Agreement was hammered out, with the union accepting it in 1960 in exchange for guaranteed hours and no layoffs. The implementation of this agreement ultimately eased the way for Seattle and other Pacific Coast ports to introduce innovations, crucially the concept of shipping goods in standardized containers.

Seattle's waterfront had been one site of early experimentation with containerization. The concept of shipping cargo in reusable, self-contained vans had several direct benefits, including being impervious to pilferage, theft, and water damage. But the key attribute was that the containers could be transferred efficiently from oceangoing vessels to trucks or trains without ever being opened — a great advance for *intermodal* shipping (using multiple modes of transportation — ship, rail, truck — to move freight). However, that very efficiency had negative ramifications for labor. At the time, a team of longshoremen could expect to get four to five days of work in unloading a typical "break-bulk" ship. With containerization, the work could be done in one day, and would require a few newly trained crane operators, rather than many strong-backed men.

CONTAINERIZATION INNOVATION

The roots of containerization extend back at least as far as the 1890s, when European and British railroads began transporting goods in wooden crates. But it took a long time for seagoing operations to follow suit. Finally, in 1929, the Seatrain company began rolling loaded railroad boxcars onto its sea vessels. And then, during World War II, the U.S. military began to transport war materiel in a form of container, which reduced the need for cargo rehandling. After the war,

in 1949, Seattle's Alaska Steamship Company innovated a commercially applicable system based on standardized six-foot wooden boxes for use on its regular Seattle-to-Alaska runs out of Pier 42.

But the real breakthrough occurred in the mid-1950s far from Puget Sound, when a North Carolina trucker named Malcolm McLean saw the lingering inefficiencies while waiting impatiently for hours as stevedores unloaded trucks' goods one armload at a time. Over the following years — while his McLean Trucking Co. grew to be the fifth-largest in the country — McLean would continue brainstorming possible solutions to that old dockside bottlenecking problem. In 1955, he sold his interest in McLean Trucking for $5 million and bought the Alabama-based Pan-Atlantic Steamship Company, which he renamed Sea-Land Industries. It was Sea-Land that, in April 1956, became the first trailblazing firm fully dedicated to the revolutionary concept of systematically hauling boxed cargo in stackable metal containers that were loaded aboard the deck of a ship. The practice proved so revolutionary in its efficiency that within one year Sea-Land overtook the dominant shipping firms of the day and vaulted to a leading position in the industry. But beyond that, McLean was so committed to the concept of global standardization within the industry that he willingly shared his legally protected container-design patents with competitors through a royalty-free lease.

ABOVE: Alaska Steamship Company pioneered its own version of containerization in 1949, starting with eight-by-eight boxes and soon moving to a standard 20-foot container.

OPPOSITE TOP: Longshore union leader Harry Bridges arrives in Seattle via a United flight, 1940s.

BELOW: Alaska Steamship Company's *Chena* in Seattle. The traditional cargo booms and winches soon gave way to designed racks that fit containers.

The Port of Seattle's commissioners were keeping a keen eye on all these developments. As at other ports, Seattle's piers and wharves were geared strictly to traditional break-bulk cargo, and it would require an enormous investment in infrastructure and equipment to change. But, in addition to containers, other big changes were fast approaching — including America's new Interstate Highway system (constructed between 1958 and 1967), which would soon be accessible by coast-to-coast trucking fleets — and Port leaders saw that they needed to fully embrace the future. With containers costing $2,000 or more each, and ships designed to carry them priced at $15 million to $25 million apiece, the costs were significant. These considerations caused certain shipping companies, and most ports, to delay making the expensive changes as long as possible. Portland in particular — because it had captured a great percentage of the West Coast's break-bulk shipping by the early 1960s — was happy with the status quo and failed to make the change that Seattle would. Portland was "unwilling to take the risk of committing the resources it took to speculate on the container business," said Richard D. Ford, executive director of the Port of Seattle from 1977 until 1985. "On the other hand, Seattle had little to lose … It had to take some risk because it was not getting the cargo; it made the decision to speculate on building facilities for containers."

CENTURY 21

In August 1962 — halfway through the six-month run (April 21–October 21) of the town's latest coming-of-age extravaganza, the Century 21 Exposition (or Seattle World's Fair) — the Port announced an ambitious $30 million terminal building program that would reclaim huge tracts of tideland along the Duwamish Waterway to build modern storage and cargo-handling facilities. In addition, the Port would undertake a six-year program to develop marginal lands and sell them to private industry in an effort to broaden Seattle's economic base. These gambles quickly paid off: By the end of the decade, Seattle had vaulted past most of its rivals to become the second-busiest container port on the West Coast.

CRANES AND COMPUTERS

The giant Sea-Land shipping company chose Seattle — specifically, the Port's new Terminal 5 across from Harbor Island on the West Waterway — as its West Coast headquarters in 1964. This partnership was a major coup for the Port, and the town soon had its first of many bright-orange container cranes reaching into the sky.

In an instance of one innovation fostering another, the efficiency of containerization soon begat the first wave of computerization. The speed of containerized freight movement made the traditional paperwork process, which had necessarily bogged down the whole shipping industry, antiquated and obsolete. Hired in 1968 by Port General Manager J. Eldon Opheim, a Port consultant named Clifford C. Muller explained that the "order of magnitude change required the paperwork not to follow the freight but, in fact, for the paperwork to 'drive' the freight. To do that there had to be up-to-the-minute,

ABOVE: Vintage Shilshole Bay Marina sign, 1963.

OPPOSITE: Over the decades, cargo handling has changed multiple times.

TOP LEFT AND RIGHT: Pallets and wooden boxes give way to cardboard boxes and mechanical gear, 1930s and 1950s.

BELOW LEFT AND RIGHT: Shear-leg derricks and ship's gear once did the work that container cranes do today.

TOP: In 1970, the roads at Sea-Tac were rerouted and parking garage construction began. Sea-Tac was a scene of nonstop activity and construction throughout the decade.

ABOVE: Fighting for equality in construction contracts, Seattle civil rights and labor leader Tyree Scott leads a protest at Sea-Tac, 1969.

real-time technology. We put up the first on-line cargo systems in 1969 [and] the first online container system in 1970; and from there implemented the online consolidation system in 1971; and finally warehousing in 1973–74."

In 1970, the Port also inked an agreement with a consortium of six Japanese containership lines — a welcome contract that established Seattle as their "first port of call" and would bring considerable Japanese goods to the West Coast. Thus, the Port's early embrace of containerization and its use of innovative trade techniques gave it a serious head start on other ports, and business boomed once again. Steady increases in trade volume, which had begun in 1963, brought numerous benefits to the region, including the generation of a great number of jobs. The Port's 1971 review of the 1960s notes Seattle harbor tonnage increased 67 percent, from nearly 11 million tons in 1958 to almost 18.4 million tons in 1969. That translated into a 193 percent increase in jobs for truckers, from 210 to 615, and a 240 percent increase in freight service jobs, from 90 to 306. The trend continued throughout the 1970s, when the Northwest experienced little other good economic news.

SEA-TAC EXPANSION: JOBS AND PROTESTS

Construction at Sea-Tac Airport through the 1960s and into the 1970s also generated well-paid jobs for the region, along with some controversy over who would get those jobs. In 1960 and 1961, the Port lengthened Sea-Tac's main runway for the third time, extending it 1,700 feet south via a bridge over South 188th Street, the airport's original boundary. Workers also enlarged the terminal, extending what are now Concourses A and D south and north from the main building, and added more parking, preparing the airport for the more than two million passengers it served in 1962, as Century 21 brought crowds of visitors to town.

By 1966, passenger volume had doubled again, and the airport and its single primary runway were rapidly approaching capacity. Attempting not just to pull even but to leap ahead of the accelerating pace of airline travel, the Port announced in 1967 an ambitious $44 million construction program (the cost would climb to $175 million before it was complete in 1973, driven in part by the high inflation of the early 1970s) to build a second north-south runway and dramatically remake the terminal's aprons and related facilities. The new 9,426-foot runway was located 800 feet west of the existing one. The narrow separation between the runways prevented their simultaneous use during periods with low clouds (some 44 percent of the time), eventually contributing to the need for a third runway.

Work on the second runway was under way in September 1969 when Sea-Tac became the scene of some of the era's more dramatic local civil rights demonstrations. Tyree Scott of the Central Contractors Association led more than 100 protestors onto the

HARBOR ISLAND AND THE DUWAMISH WATERWAYS

HARBOR ISLAND

From ancient times the Duwamish River — whose mouth at Elliott Bay was originally forked by a small cluster of low marshy islands — was the lifeblood of the Duwamish tribe. The river's banks were home for numerous villages; its flowing waters were rich with salmon and herring runs and provided an inland transportation route for canoes. The largest of those estuarial islands was ćəqas ("Muddy" or "Something Dirty"), which had long been excellent for deer hunting. In time the soggy land was settled by a chicken rancher named Charles Butler who, failing to file the requisite land-claim paperwork, eventually was forced to vacate.

In 1900, the Seattle General Construction Co. began tideland reclamation by filling the tideflats at the mouth of the river. Then Puget Sound Bridge & Dredging Co. dredged the river to deepen the channel and dumped the spoils onto ceqas, which would become Harbor Island. The firm also used placer-mining technology to sluice soil in large pipes from the Jackson Hill and Dearborn Street regrade projects. After piling up 24 million cubic yards of soil, work was completed in 1909 and the resultant 350-acre area would be, for two decades, the world's largest artificial island.

Harbor Island soon became the home of various private industrial enterprises including the ca. 1911, Fisher Flouring Mills; Associated Shipyards (which constructed steamships during World War I); and Todd Shipyards, which arrived in 1918. In 1926, the Fisher family founded KOMO radio in a broadcasting station behind their mill. In 1933 they acquired Seattle's premier station, KJR, and in 1936 a modern steel radio tower was erected on Harbor Island.

Squeezed for space after the U.S. military took over Seattle's central waterfront during World War II, in 1942 the Port of Seattle purchased the East Waterway Dock on Harbor Island for $900,000. Development of the island continued — in 1967 the Port expanded it to 396 acres — but the years had taken their toll on its environmental health. In 1983, the Environmental Protection Agency (EPA) — citing tests showing lead-smelting contamination — placed Harbor Island on the National Priority List of polluted sites. The Port decontaminated various areas and continues to monitor the site. Today Harbor Island is home to Todd Pacific Shipyards, a Burlington Northern Santa Fe railyard, several petroleum terminals, and the Port's Piers 16 and 17, the 106-acre Terminal 18 container facility, and Terminals 10 and 102.

WEST WATERWAY

The western bank of the Duwamish River was the site of several traditional villages of the Duwamish peoples, including ha'àh'pus ("Where There Are Horse Clams"), located just north of the Port of Seattle's Terminal 107. The largest one, tuʔəlàlʔtxʷ ("Herring's House"), was at the river's original mouth at Elliott Bay, under today's Spokane Street bridge.

The Port's Terminal 5 is now located on the west bank of the waterway. Decades of unregulated industrial use by Pacific Sound Resources and Lockheed Shipbuilding resulted in the EPA designating the area a Superfund cleanup site. The Port undertook a massive cleanup effort in 1997. Additional expansion of Port facilities on the site spurred the initiation of a multiyear program in June 2008 that led to remediation efforts scheduled to be completed by 2012. Just upstream, the Port runs Terminals 103 and 115, a major barge terminal for goods shipped to Alaska.

EAST WATERWAY

The eastern river bank featured a promontory that was the site of a Duwamish village named tətalxʷqs ("Little Strong Point") that had been used as a defensive refuge. Nearby was a traditional native work station, dəxʷpačəb ("Place For Setting Things Out"). By the 1890s there was a push to excavate a water passageway that would connect Elliott Bay with Lake Washington. While some believed the best route would be via Salmon Bay and Lake Union, others thought cutting through the northern part of Beacon Hill was the answer, and some preferred the Duwamish River. By 1896, Eugene Semple's company had excavated the East Waterway 2,000 feet upstream from Elliott Bay, built bulkheads, and filled in about 50 acres of tidelands — but after much debate, the "South Canal" project was halted in favor of the "North Canal" at Salmon Bay.

During World War II, the Port augmented its Hanford Street Grain Terminal with a major new elevator that in time brought increased business activity. Development continued and today the Port owns Terminals 30, 46, 104, 106, and 108 in this area. Sediments here have been declared a Superfund cleanup site and a multiyear program was initiated in May 2010.

LEFT: Postcard view of Fisher Flouring Mills on Harbor Island, 1914.

TOP: Five ships dock at Pier 20, today's Terminal 18, with Seattle's Space Needle in the background, ca. 1970s.

ABOVE: Aerial of Harbor Island and East Waterway, 1967.

airport's flight apron, delaying some flights and shutting down construction. That action and a sit-in at the airport terminal in November were part of a campaign by African American contractors and workers to win a share of federally funded construction projects and jobs ($47 million for Sea-Tac construction came from the federal government). Although the Port and other agencies were amenable, the powerful building trades unions, which largely controlled hiring, resisted calls to open lucrative skilled construction jobs to minorities. Federal District Judge William J. Lindberg prohibited further disruption, but six months later he found the unions in violation of the 1964 Civil Rights Act and imposed a sweeping affirmative action program on the construction industry, including quotas in hiring, training, and union membership. Despite the turmoil, the second runway was completed in September 1970, and work on rebuilding and expanding terminal facilities continued even as the bottom dropped out of the regional economy.

THE BOEING BUST

As the 1960s flowed into the 1970s, the national aerospace industry took a nosedive. Earlier estimates — which projected that the skyrocketing trend-lines of air passenger usage seen between 1955 and 1965 would continue — had been in error. Moreover, since the Northwest region's largest single employer was The Boeing Company, Seattle's economy was hit particularly hard. Just as demand for the 747 model began to slow, the U.S. Congress voted to end its decadelong support for Boeing's supersonic transport (SST) project. Boeing's roster slid from a peak of 100,800 employees in 1967 to a low of 38,690 in April 1971. Whereas Seattle had recently boasted an unemployment rate under the national average, it instantly soared above 12 percent — the highest in the nation and the worst of any major American city since the Great Depression. This recession — known locally as the "Boeing Bust" — saw perhaps 10,000 people moving away to find work. Seattle's problems gained national headlines when two enterprising real-estate agents famously contracted to have a billboard near Sea-Tac Airport display the darkly humorous message: "Will the last person leaving SEATTLE — Turn out the lights?"

Soon after that "sign of the times" garnered national media attention, a new organization formed to counter the notion that Seattle was facing economic collapse. The King County Economic Development Council launched a $2 million advertising campaign designed to play up the good news — and the centerpiece of its message touted the vitality of the Port. But beyond influencing the national audience, this spotlighting of the Port's contributions to the local economy and community also vastly increased the public's knowledge of and appreciation for the Port.

Times had certainly changed. Only 10 years earlier, the Port of Seattle had been, as historian Padraic Burke noted, "scorned and derided as the most backward and crisis-prone port on the West Coast." Now the agency was increasingly seen as a potential savior of the city's future. Boeing began to recover in fits and starts, but it was growth at the Port that helped ease the regional downturn. Among the projects launched during those times was the $25 million purchase of the historic Boeing Plant 1 site — a 25-acre parcel two miles up the Duwamish Waterway that would be developed into a major new facility, Terminal 115. In addition, the old Hanford Street grain elevator was transformed into a large $8 million fully modernized container terminal.

ARCHITECTURE AND ART AT SEA-TAC

Of all the Port projects during the 1970s, it was probably the rebuilding and expansion of Sea-Tac that most affected the public. Work continued steadily, and in July 1973, as air traffic rebounded (5.2 million travelers passed through Sea-Tac that year), the Port unveiled its new terminals and ancillary facilities to general praise. The redevelopment encased the 1949 administration building inside a dramatic new structure featuring vehicle access via an upper drive for departures and a lower level for baggage claim and arrivals. Sky bridges connected the main terminal to a multi-deck parking garage.

Satellite terminals were added north and south of the main building, which passengers reached via a pair of subway loops equipped with driverless automatic shuttle trains. This train was the first of its kind in the nation and opened in 1973 with nine cars. Other improvements included new facilities for fuel, air cargo, and aircraft maintenance. The Port also commissioned $300,000 worth of new works by major local, national, and international artists for the terminal. The unprecedented display — the first of its kind in any U.S. airport — was the beginning of the Port's public art collection, which grew to include significant art works throughout public areas and offices at the airport, in the Port's waterfront headquarters, and at other properties.

ABOVE: Seattle Mayor J. D. Braman greets President Lyndon Johnson at Sea-Tac Airport in 1966.

OPPOSITE TOP LEFT: President John Kennedy visits Seattle on September 27, 1963. Journalists and a crowd of onlookers watch as he walks with Senator Warren Magnuson to a helicopter.

TOP RIGHT: Robert Kennedy addresses a crowd of supporters at Sea-Tac, March 26, 1968.

CHANGING TIMES

Rapidly changing times are unsettling, and the political, economic, and cultural revolutions of the 1960s and '70s were a kaleidoscopic whirlwind. Faced daily with the inescapable evidence of change, the newly buoyant Port was soon hearing from a range of critics. A major emerging issue — especially in the wake of the high-profile nationwide events held on the first annual Earth Day (April 22, 1970) — was the declining state of the environment. Two major points of contention embodied the basic conflict: the issue of noise levels around Sea-Tac Airport and the Port's erection of what was to be the last bulk terminal facility ever built on the Elliott Bay waterfront.

Even before the new Sea-Tac terminal opened, residents in nearby communities were complaining of noise levels caused by increasing jet traffic. Almost 7,000 people petitioned the Port to buy out approximately 2,000 homes in Zone Three, the Federal Aviation Administration–designated area where noise levels were highest. Other residents sued the Port for reduced property value, cracked windows and plaster, and frayed nerves, winning millions in compensation. Seeking a comprehensive solution, the Port and King County — with support and funding from the FAA — began preparing what became known as the Sea-Tac Communities Plan in January 1973. Adopted in 1976, the plan created the nation's first large-scale program to reduce noise impacts by acquiring property outside airport boundaries, as the Port agreed to buy or insulate the homes most affected by aircraft noise. Acquisition proceeded steadily and the Port won several awards for the program, but affected neighbors continued to complain about noise and about the slow pace of insulating their homes.

The controversially massive $13 million Pier 86 Grain Terminal arose bayside in 1970 at the foot of Queen Anne Hill, a long-established neighborhood whose residents treasured their views across Puget Sound. Those views were now marred by a towering industrial edifice that was much more imposing than the original 1967 proposal plans depicted. Other issues included the facility's daily clouds of wafting grain-dust and the loud clanking of railroad cars. Although a public relations problem, the facility was a grand economic success. The modern, automated structure (with a 4.2 million metric ton storage capacity) also boasted a deep-water shipping pier — a pairing that was unmatched on the West Coast.

The new grain terminal was great for Port business but not a big enough factor to quiet critics. Citizen complaints led to hearings in Olympia before the legislature's Committee on Local Government, where a stream of individuals denounced the Port as "aloof" and "unresponsive" to the concerns of local communities. Then, in March 1974, a referendum was held on a proposal to block a project that the Port deemed crucial to marine development on its properties — the financing of a high-rise bridge from I-5 over the Duwamish Waterway to West Seattle. The proposal failed, but it brought about some beneficial soul-searching at the Port. Merle Adlum convinced his fellow commissioners that it was time to commit to being more attuned to community ethics and environmental

ABOVE TOP: A whirly crane rotates and loads containers on a ship at Terminal 46, 1973.

ABOVE: As part of a public access program, the Port opened a fishing pier at Pier 57 in 1968. It was replaced in 1981 by the fishing pier at Terminal 86. The Port now operates 22 parks and public access areas.

OPPOSITE: Seattle waterfront, looking north along the East Waterway, ca. 1965.

Once a cold storage and fish processing site, Terminal 25 became a container terminal occupied by AML, later American President Lines (APL), as shown in this 1976 photo. APL later moved to Terminal 5.

concerns. One example of their heightened sensitivity to such matters was the steps commissioners took to mitigate the Pier 86 grain terminal problems: Pollution controls were added, its grounds were nicely landscaped, and public pedestrian and bicycling paths were installed.

Meanwhile, the challenges the Port faced in balancing its multiple roles in the community were considerable and complicated. It was growth at the Port, after all, that had largely kept the local economy afloat in recent years, and Port leadership knew that it must continue being aggressive to maintain momentum against other ports. Certainly, it was undeniable that competition was heating up again. Although the Port of Seattle had surged ahead of it in the 1960s, the Port of Tacoma succeeded in luring Totem Ocean Trailer Express (TOTE) — a major shipper to Alaska —away from Seattle, partially because the land surrounding the Port of Tacoma was valued at far less than Seattle's and it could easily offer TOTE room to expand. Stung by the loss, the Port of Seattle set out to acquire more than $1.5 million worth of additional land to expand terminals along both sides of the Duwamish Waterway. Other facility enhancements also were planned, including constructing a container freight station at Terminal 25 for APL (one of its biggest carrier customers) and a building for the assembly of imported cars at Terminal 115. The Port also purchased an additional 8.5 acres at Terminal 28, where the Nissan Line would deliver containers and steel — and automobiles. Auto manufacturer Datsun (Nissan)

ABOVE: Imported cars at Terminal 91, 1982. Tens of thousands of cars entered the U.S. through Seattle during the 1970s and 1980s.

LEFT: The *Liu Lin Hai*, the first Chinese ship to enter a U.S. port in 30 years, loads grain at Terminal 86 in April 1979. A public pathway runs beside the Terminal 86 Grain Facility.

declared Seattle its "point of entry" for automobiles destined for the Midwestern and East Coast markets. (Terminals 25 and 28 have since been incorporated into Terminal 30.)

In 1975 — in a sort of one-step-back, two steps-forward shuffle — longtime Port user United Brands suddenly announced that it would end four decades of making weekly banana boat calls, opting instead to transport its product via rail and trucks. But that same year, the Japan Six-Line shipping consortium added vessels that doubled its container capacity, and the Port offered the firm use of Terminal 37 at decade's end. Then in 1976 the Port reacquired the 198-acre Terminal 91 facility (Piers 90 and 91 at Smith

ABOVE: The captain and officers of the *Liu Lin Hai* disembark at Terminal 91, April 18, 1979.

RIGHT: Port Commissioner Jack Block peers over the shoulder of Commissioner Henry Kotkins (second from right) to join Senator Henry Jackson (center), Chinese officials, and the captain of the *Liu Lin Hai* in celebrating the ship's arrival in Seattle, April 18, 1979.

Cove) from the U.S. Navy and subsequently devoted it to cold storage for seafood exports to Japan and other Asian markets.

Another international breakthrough occurred in 1979 when President Jimmy Carter's administration announced the opening of full diplomatic ties with the People's Republic of China — a move long advocated by U.S. Senator Warren G. Magnuson of Washington. That April, maritime history was made when a Chinese-owned cargo ship — the *Liu Lin Hai* — cruised into Puget Sound and docked at Pier 91. The 637-foot, Norwegian-built ship brought no cargo, but it left Seattle with 37,000 metric tons of corn from the Midwest that it loaded at the Pier 86 grain terminal. The historic event ended a 30-year trade embargo and established Seattle as the first U.S. port to host a vessel from the country that would eventually become the Port's largest import trade partner.

Following the end of the Vietnam War in 1975, there was further evolution in Asian trade markets, and the Port of Seattle was among the first to send trade representatives to Vietnam to discuss opportunities. But at the same time, a new business model was emerging for imported goods that placed a premium on how close a harbor was to population centers where cargo could be sold. Under this model, Seattle's efficiency as a hub of intermodal transport was no longer as persuasive as it once had been. Instead, emerging Asian exporters were powerfully attracted to the idea of shipping to the ports of Los Angeles and Long Beach, which offered not only an immediate market of 7 million consumers for their goods, but also train and truck connections to the rest of the country. King County's population of 1.1 million simply could not compete with Southern California.

A significant parallel development was under way, as the Carter administration persuaded Congress in 1978 to deregulate the airline industry, allowing carriers to

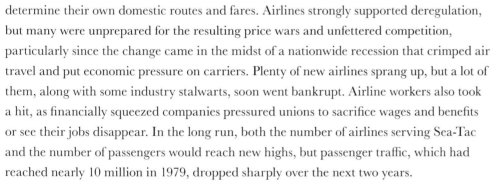

determine their own domestic routes and fares. Airlines strongly supported deregulation, but many were unprepared for the resulting price wars and unfettered competition, particularly since the change came in the midst of a nationwide recession that crimped air travel and put economic pressure on carriers. Plenty of new airlines sprang up, but a lot of them, along with some industry stalwarts, soon went bankrupt. Airline workers also took a hit, as financially squeezed companies pressured unions to sacrifice wages and benefits or see their jobs disappear. In the long run, both the number of airlines serving Sea-Tac and the number of passengers would reach new highs, but passenger traffic, which had reached nearly 10 million in 1979, dropped sharply over the next two years.

A new era was dawning that would at once challenge the Port of Seattle to reinvent itself yet again and cause the people of Seattle to reimagine their beloved town and begin planning for its rapid emergence as a truly world-class city.

LEFT: Air cargo through Sea-Tac has increased annually since 1955. Here, a China Airlines aircraft is loaded, 1980.

ABOVE: Special supplement published in community newspapers in July 1973, celebrating Sea-Tac Airport's 25th anniversary.

GOVERNOR DAN EVANS WELCOMES VIETNAMESE REFUGEES

It was early morning in the spring of 1975 when Washington Governor Dan Evans caught a news broadcast that California's Governor Jerry Brown was opposing the resettlement of Vietnamese refugees in his state.

The Vietnam War ended April 30th with the fall of Saigon to the communists. U.S. Secretary of State Henry Kissinger wanted funding to care for as many as 70,000 refugees. Thousands were taken to California, but Brown didn't want them there. One of Brown's aides even tried to keep the first airplane from landing.

Evans, a Republican, was incensed. How could a Democratic governor be so heartless? "This was not the attitude we wanted associated with our state," Evans told *The New York Times*. He was determined to show the governor of California, a state 2.3 times larger than Washington, how Washingtonians would lead the way.

Evans sent assistant Ralph Munro to Camp Pendleton where thousands of Vietnamese families were being temporarily held. "He said, 'If you see that goddamn Jerry Brown, remind him what it says on the bottom of the Statue of Liberty,'" Munro recalled to *The Seattle Times*.

A tablet at the base of the Statue of Liberty on Ellis Island, where millions of immigrants arrived in the U.S., reads: "Give me your tired, your poor, your huddled masses yearning to breathe free, the wretched refuse of your teeming shore. Send these, the homeless, tempest-tossed to me, I lift my lamp beside the golden door!"

Sure, there was opposition in Washington state. But Evans, arguably the best leader in state history, would overcome that. "This is a genuine national challenge," he told a reporter that year. "It's really not all that tough. And yet it helps so many people directly."

TOP LEFT: Governor Dan Evans greets refugees Tony Le and his son at Camp Murray, May 20, 1975.

ABOVE AND OPPOSITE: When "Operation Baby Lift" arrived at Sea-Tac a little after 2 a.m. on April 7, 1975, immigration officials worked throughout the night to make sure the children received proper care.

When the first 34 Vietnamese arrived at Sea-Tac to a cheering crowd the afternoon of May 20, 1975, Evans greeted them in their native language. These steps, Evans said earlier that day, were a moral responsibility. By the end of September, nearly 1,400 had been placed through the state program that initially housed refugees at Camp Murray.

The airport was where hundreds of Vietnamese children met their new families even before the start of the refugee resettlement program.

The first plane of Vietnamese refugees landed at Sea-Tac at 12:37 a.m. April 6, 1975, less than a month before the fall of Saigon. Adoptive parents lined the windows of Concourse A hours ahead of the flight's arrival. When the Pan-Am flight touched down with 414 children and 67 adults, parents held pictures of their new children and workers from an Oregon-based service agency introduced them, matching the children with numbers on their plastic bracelets.

Among the orphans was a 4-month-old girl who'd been found abandoned outside the Vietnamese capitol. She was evacuated on a U.S. Air Force cargo plane, but four days before her arrival at Sea-Tac that cargo plane crashed while trying to make an emergency landing. She was among the few survivors, though her identifying paperwork was burned in the crash.

When the infant met her new parents at Sea-Tac "the four-month-old Vietnamese orphan girl didn't even raise an eyelid as Western Airlines chaperone Marge Franklin placed the infant in the arms of her new parents, John and Lana Mitsules," the Post-Intelligencer reported. "It is possible that she was the youngest to survive the crash near Saigon that killed about 178 persons, most of them Vietnamese orphans."

The willingness of Washingtonians to help, and Evans' actions to create the refugee resettlement program, made the Evergreen State the first state to step forward, establishing a model that would continue for decades.

President Gerald Ford later asked Evans to serve on a presidential advisory committee on Vietnamese refugees. Recalling that service, Evans remembered Ford's remarks at the opening meeting: "Most, if not all, of us are the beneficiaries of the opportunities that come from a country that has an open door. In one way or another, all of us are immigrants. And the strength of America over the years has been our diversity ..."

Evans noted that many U.S. citizens vehemently opposed giving haven to an enemy we fought so bitterly. But he wrote that the Vietnamese refugees he had welcomed to Washington were innocent people fleeing the excesses of a new regime.

Evans wrote in 2014 that he was "exceedingly proud of the volunteer sponsors, support organizations and legislators who welcomed these productive new citizens to our state." He noted Washington state has the third-largest Vietnamese population in the U.S., behind California and Texas.

"We cannot forever huddle fearfully behind high gray walls," Evans wrote in The Seattle Times. "That is not the America I know. Instead, let us celebrate our diversity that makes us strong."

Chapter 6: **COMPETITION AND EXPANSION**

The sluggish global economy of the 1970s had presented significant hurdles to the leaders of many industries — including interconnected ones, such as ports, steamship lines, railroads, trucking companies, and airlines. However, due in great measure to the leadership at the Port of Seattle, which had kept its eyes on the prize — the rapidly modernizing economies of various Asian countries — the Pacific Northwest suffered less than some areas. And when the Pacific Rim boom erupted in full force during the 1980s, careful preparations had positioned Seattle to capitalize on the increased trade. A visionary concept took hold that saw Seattle as a "crossroads" city strategically located between Asia and Europe.

OPPOSITE: The derelict condition of the central waterfront, shown in 1986, led the Port to embark on a major redevelopment and revival of the area.

Piers 64, 65, and 66 were torn down to make room for the first of the central waterfront redevelopment projects, the new Bell Street Pier, 1995.

BUILDING A WORLD-CLASS CITY

The notion that it was Seattle's rightful destiny to be recognized as a world-class city was long held by many residents and business leaders. The Port would be instrumental in achieving that goal by sparking general business growth, which would attract the waves of incoming population required for a metropolis to reach critical mass. It took the creative contributions of many individuals and companies to turn the dream into reality.

Innovative new local companies, such as Microsoft and Starbucks, joined forces with such established heavyweights as Boeing, Weyerhaeuser, and PACCAR to help catapult Seattle into the big leagues. Improved attractions along the central waterfront, major-league sports, and the arts also helped. Real estate values soared, investors and developers bought in, and the city's skyline was quickly altered with scores of new high-rise office and residential buildings. Perhaps the most visible change fostered by the Port during the 1980s was along Seattle's central waterfront. An area decades in decline, the waterfront was about to see a major upgrade — in both public amenities and harbor facilities. Throughout the 1980s, the Port invested an unprecedented $512 million in a massive modernization and expansion program.

AIR CARGO AT SEA AIRPORT

From their earliest days, airplanes have carried goods as well as people. Indeed cargo — specifically United States mail — played a critical role in the development of both commercial airplanes and passenger airlines. The Boeing Company got its start building warplanes for the U.S. military during World War I, but when the war ended the new company nearly went broke — until Boeing test pilot Eddie Hubbard demonstrated the viability of transporting mail by air when he and Bill Boeing flew to Canada and returned with America's first international airmail delivery. Within months the U.S. Post Office (now the Postal Service) began granting contracts for scheduled airmail service to private companies, many flying Boeing planes. Air travel grew as more and more passengers rode on the mail planes and Boeing went on to develop powerful new planes. At Hubbard's urging, Boeing also bid for and won the Post Office's lucrative Chicago to San Francisco mail route. The air transport unit that Boeing created to serve the route grew into airline behemoth United Air Lines.

By the time Seattle-Tacoma International Airport (Sea-Tac, now knowns as SEA Airport) was dedicated in 1949, United and the other airlines serving it concentrated largely on passenger service, carrying a relatively small amount of mail and other cargo (just over 6,000 tons in 1950, Sea-Tac's first full year of operation) in the bellies of their passenger liners. The airport's first cargo-only carrier — Flying Tiger Line, many of whose pilots had "flown the hump" ferrying troops and supplies over the Himalayas during World War II — arrived in 1952. Mail was still a big part of air cargo, and just as the Post Office had earlier given Boeing and United a leg up, it helped boost Sea-Tac's cargo business by designating it in 1956 as the airport for shipping all first-class mail to Asia from west of the Mississippi. The Post Office airmail facility built the next year saw huge increases in airmail from Sea-Tac to Southeast Asia as U.S. involvement in the Vietnam War increased. Total air cargo rose to 48,660 tons in 1964, doubled to 96,437 tons in 1967, and jumped another 30 percent to 123,577 tons in 1968.

Airmail volume dropped sharply as the Vietnam War wound down and the airmail center was eventually moved to San Francisco, bringing temporary declines in total cargo shipped through Sea-Tac. However, other types of air cargo continued to grow. During the 1960s, high quality,

low weight freight and highly perishable items were increasingly carried in the bellies of passenger planes. In addition, by the early 1970s, two more cargo-only carriers joined Flying Tiger (which was later purchased by FedEx). The Port of Seattle added air cargo facilities during the 1970s and then doubled cargo-handling capacity in the early 1980s with a new air cargo center. The Port's cargo program —seamlessly unloading Asian container ships and rushing the cargo to airplanes for immediate flight to European markets— proved particularly successful. In 1990, Sea-Tac ranked first worldwide in volume of sea-air cargo.

Among the wide variety of cargos are some iconic representatives of the region SEA Airport serves. Since 1984, when Northwest Airlines carried the first shipment of local cherries to South Korea, Sea-Tac exports jump dramatically each summer as 25 to 30 million pounds of fresh Washington cherries are shipped to Korea and Taiwan for distribution throughout Asia. Spare parts for Washington-made Boeing planes are also part of the airport's air cargo — since it opened in 1993, Boeing's Spares Distribution Center has shipped millions of parts to customers around the world, keeping the global aircraft fleet aloft.

Between 2015 and 2020, the Port partnered with private developers to build/lease more than 2.2 million square feet of light space industrial near SEA Airport. Electric and industrial machinery were the top exports at $4.7 billion combined, and industrial machinery and electronic integrated circuits were the top imports at more than $4.2 billion.

In 2020, after nine consecutive years of air cargo growth, SEA Airport moved 454,584 metric tons of air cargo, almost matching the 457,071 metric ton record set in 2000. Twenty-seven carriers serve the airport, including freighter services and cargo carried on passenger jets. With globally recognized companies including Microsoft, Amazon, Costco, Starbucks, Phillips, Nordstrom, Expedia, and Weyerhaeuser, SEA plays a vital role in the productivity and growth of businesses that call the Puget Sound home and is an economic engine that facilitates the region's economy.

FROM TOP: Flying Tiger Air Cargo, 1970s; Loading logs, 1985; Northwest cherries destined for China, 2001; Alaska Air Cargo, 2010.

D.B. COOPER

ABOVE: FBI sketches of Cooper

OPPOSITE: Flight attendant Tina Mucklow, pictured here after the event, played a primary role in communicating with Cooper throughout the hijacking.

BELOW: The ticket was filled out for "Dan" Cooper, not "D. B." Cooper as a *United Press International* reporter initially announced. The story took off so fast that even with a correction, the D.B. name stuck.

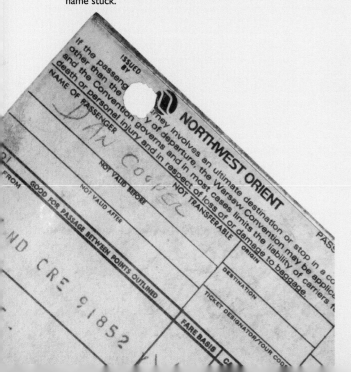

It was the day before Thanksgiving, November 24, 1971, when a man in a black suit and tie approached an airport counter in Portland and paid $20 cash for a one-way ticket to Seattle-Tacoma International Airport.

He seemed like any normal passenger in his 40s at the time, signing his name in red ink and sitting alone awaiting the short flight. He sat in the flight's last row, drinking a bourbon and soda and not drawing attention until he passed a flight attendant a handwritten note. She figured it was a pickup attempt until the man in horn-rimmed sunglasses told her to read it.

"I have a bomb."

More than a half century later, it remains the nation's only unsolved airplane hijacking.

The all-caps name on his ticket read Dan Cooper. But when the United Press International wire service was rushing to move the story, the hijacker was mistakenly listed as D. B. Cooper. The FBI corrected it the next day in a press release, but by that time the error had already traveled around the world, and the D. B. moniker stuck.

In the air, flight attendant Tina Mucklow sat next to Cooper at his request. He opened a briefcase to show wires, a battery, and red sticks. He wanted $200,000 – roughly $1.5 million in 2024 dollars – waiting when he landed. If Cooper got the money and parachutes, the 36 passengers and all but one flight attendant and the pilots could go.

During its first decades, the airport relied on guides for both security and customer service, the norm at domestic airports then. The guides, in green uniforms and ranger-style caps, would keep unauthorized people off the loading ramps, check on building lights, man vehicles and two-way radio contact with the control tower, and help reunite lost children.

There were other hijackings connected to the airport, including the first attempt in 1954 when an armed man climbed aboard a DC-3 awaiting takeoff and demanded to be flown to Africa. The airport's chief security guard, Marvin Stansel, convinced him to surrender before anyone was hurt. But it was the night in November 1971 that showed the need for a Port police force, long before it was mandated by the FAA. Said Oris Dunham, former director of the Port's Aviation Division, "It all started with D. B. Cooper."

The FBI rushed to get the money while an airport manager procured four parachutes from an Issaquah sky-diving school. Cooper also wanted a fuel truck waiting. The flight crew on the Boeing 727 was told to fly to Mexico. Not long after takeoff, Cooper had the rear stairs extended. About 20 miles north of Portland – the FBI can't pinpoint exactly where – Cooper jumped. The plane was going 196 mph and was roughly 10,000 feet high. The wind chill was well below zero at that altitude when Cooper jumped.

Whether Cooper survived or not wasn't the issue for airport security. What he'd done – exposing a terrorism risk in an era long before rigorous pre-screening protocols – showed a weakness and a need. Speaking in 2021, Mucklow, the last person to see or speak to Cooper, told *Rolling Stone* she believes the Cooper hijacking was the start of a dangerous turning point, the start of an escalation in hijackings that culminated in the 9/11 attacks.

On December 14, 1971, less than a month after Cooper's hijacking, port commissioners authorized the establishment of an airport-specific police department at the request of Aviation Director Donald G. Shay. Port Legal Officer Richard Ford told the commissioners that initial transformation into a police department "will mean only a change of officers' badges," because the 27 men deputized to work at the airport by the King County Director of Public Safety were already funded by the Port.

The federal government followed, mandating that airports have an accredited police force. In 1973, the FAA mandated armed guards at checkpoints leading to an additional 35 provisional officers. A waterfront division was also formed that year to address cargo theft. (The Port of Seattle Fire Department was formed July 5, 1955, and the first fire station was completed four years later.)

A Port resolution in 1974 expanded the powers of the police department to include all Port-owned properties, and the department name officially became the Port of Seattle Police Department. Former Assistant Seattle Police Chief Neil Moloney was hired the following year. He started a K9 unit and bomb squad. Moloney led the department until 1981 when Governor John Spellman tapped him to lead the State Patrol.

On the night of Cooper's flight, the airport averaged around 14,000 daily passengers. By 2023, that number was more than 50,000. Department capabilities grew to include a dive team, marine patrol, traffic support, a civil disturbance unit, participation on the Joint Terrorism Task Force, a regional SWAT force, hostage negotiators, and its own fire and police dispatch center. A half century after its creation, the Port of Seattle Police Department had 130 officers and another 47 non-commissioned staff.

The Cooper manhunt in southwest Washington continued for months, and the case became a legend for people growing up in the Northwest. Letters, some with each letter cut from different fonts, were mailed anonymously by people claiming to be the hijacker. There were folk songs and

made-for-TV movies. More than one man made a deathbed confession.

In February 1980, an 8-year-old boy vacationing with his family found three bundles of deteriorated $20 bills, still bound with rubber bands. Fascination was reignited when the FBI confirmed it was Cooper's money. Every year since the hijacking, there have been news stories of people claiming to be Cooper or being certain about his identity. As the Internet and social media developed, the FBI posted case records and photos asking for tips.

The eight Raleigh filter-tipped cigarette butts Cooper smoked before he jumped might have been good sources for DNA evidence. But, like the black tie he wore that day, that led to only a partial DNA sample in 2001, many other people made contact with them. And the cigarette butts, which fit into a worn cardboard box at the FBI's Seattle field office in 2009, disappeared from the remaining Cooper evidence.

In 2016, the bureau announced they were no longer actively investigating the Cooper hijacking, code named NORJACK. Spokesperson Ayn Dietrich-Williams called it "one of the longest and most exhaustive investigations in our history," but said the resources were needed for other investigative priorities.

As for Cooper's true identity? That depends on who you ask.

"There's this idea of a debonair guy," said Geoffrey Gray, author of the *New York Times* best seller *Skyjack: The Hunt for D. B. Cooper.* But his tie was a clip-on from JCPenney. His suit didn't match his pants. He didn't demand large bills, so the FBI gave small denominations to add extra weight. Investigators doubt he realized that one of the four parachutes was sewn shut. "The man," Gray told CBS News, "is probably nothing like the myth."

ABOVE TOP: Cappy Thompson's stained-glass window "I Was Dreaming of Spirit Animals" was installed in Concourse A in 2004. In 1969, the Port dedicated $300,000 for art at Sea-Tac and was the first public agency in the region to establish a public art collection. The Port's Public Art Program continues to grow and evolve, and the region's diversity is well-represented through European, Asian, Northwest Native American, and folk-art influences. Some of the works are by 20th century artists of great renown, such as Frank Stella, Louise Nevelson, and Robert Rauschenberg.

ABOVE: Double-stacked rail cars doubled the amount of cargo a train could carry. These new cars were introduced in the mid-1980s.

CONTAINERIZATION (PART 2) AND COMPETITION

Thanks to the foresight of Port leadership, the second containerization revolution, sparked by the railroad industry, paid long-lasting dividends to the local economy. The railroads had come to realize they could double the number of containers hauled on their flatcars simply by stacking the metal boxes two-high. This novel idea, while providing remarkable gains in efficiency, also required expensive design changes to containers, along with the reconstruction of many bridges, crossings, and other facilities to make room for the higher loads (some, like the Stampede Pass tunnel in the Cascade mountain range, have yet to be enlarged). The Port itself needed to invest considerable sums in converting its terminals to accommodate these changes.

Another major development came in the 1980s, when one of the world's largest shipping firms, APL (formerly called American President Lines Ltd.), commissioned the construction of $100 million C-10 vessels, which, as a class, became known as "post-Panamax" ships. The name derived from the fact that for decades most oceangoing freighters had been limited to less that 1,000 feet long and 91 feet wide — dimensions imposed by the physical limits of the Panama Canal locks. Now, with railroads and trucking providing efficient transcontinental transport for most goods, APL instead committed to building giant ships that couldn't pass through the Canal, but, by carrying up to 30 percent more cargo, would work well on the lucrative trans-Pacific trade routes.

At the same time, competition sharpened with other ports, both distant and near. Having embraced containerization later than Seattle, the Port of Tacoma aggressively marketed its new container and dockside intermodal facilities in the 1980s, including on-dock rail spurs that allowed loading of containers directly onto flatcars. Sea-Land became the first of several container lines to move operations from Seattle to Tacoma. Later, Tacoma also lured away former Port of Seattle customers K-Line and Evergreen Marine Corp. of Taiwan. This keen competition — and the perception that shipping lines were playing the ports against each other — led to increasing calls to merge the two Puget Sound ports or create a state port authority.

Despite such competition, the Port of Seattle continued to grow and to foster regional economic development. But the role of the agency had evolved to such an extent that Port leadership realized the larger community had a diminished sense of what the Port actually *did*. No longer just the destination or transshipment point it had been in earlier years, the Port was, in essence, now a landlord and a builder of transportation infrastructure, and that was harder to package in an easily understood concept. So, as the Port's role evolved, its leaders thought the public no longer fully understood or necessarily

supported desired initiatives. Perhaps that helps explain why on November 8, 1983, area voters elected to the Seattle Port Commission a candidate whose whole campaign amounted to a publicity gag: the local seafood restaurateur and celebrity Ivar Haglund.

THE PACIFIC RIM

Business was booming. After the call of the *Liu Lin Hai*, a massive new market opened for the Port of Seattle. In 1980, a delegation headed by Lin Zuyi from the China Ocean Shipping Company (COSCO) arrived and began forging a relationship with the Port. Soon thereafter, the Port of Shanghai sent four managers to participate in a three-month training internship at the Port, and upon their return, they set out to successfully develop China's first container terminal at the Port of Shanghai. From there, the business interactions between the two nations grew splendidly: A U.S.–China trade level of only $4.81 billion in 1980 soared to $366 billion two decades later.

The 1980s also made intermodal connections increasingly important — particularly dockside rail lines — and the Port's efforts to accommodate demand paid off. During that decade, Seattle's waterfront saw further development and ever-higher shipping activity. Companies central to this growth included China Ocean Shipping Co. (which nearly doubled its capacity by adding two more dedicated ships); Evergreen (which increased its activity by 40 percent); Hanjin Shipping Co. of South Korea (which added larger vessels to increase capacity by 40 percent); and U.S.–based Matson Navigation Co. (which doubled its capacity).

By decade's end, the Port was handling more than 1 million containers per year. And with labor and management committed to working more closely together, a new record for container crane productivity was set in 1989. In some cases, the growth in traffic was a direct result of the Port providing improved marine facilities to help ensure the competitive position of its customers. For example, in 1985, the Port completed one of its crown jewels: a $12 million expansion of its Terminal 106 national distribution center (which was followed in 1986 by another $9 million augmentation). This facility became the successful home for one of the world's largest toy manufacturing companies, Hasbro Inc., which made Seattle its sole port of entry for containerized shipments from Asia.

Similarly, when videogame maker Nintendo Co. Ltd. of Kyoto, Japan, moved its U.S. operations (Nintendo of America, Inc.) from New York City to King County (Redmond, Washington) in 1982, the company cited the area's transportation and Port facilities as contributing to its decision. Other advances at the Port included the investment of $50 million in redeveloping the 77-acre Terminal 5 facility. The Port also invested $3.9 million in preparing Terminal 25 for Matson, and improved and expanded

ABOVE: In 1983, businessman and local personality Ivar Haglund (of Ivar's Seafood Restaurants) ran for Port Commission as a publicity stunt. To his surprise, he was elected and held the seat from 1984 to 1985.

BELOW: Loading wheat seed, 1984.

ABOVE: Terminal 46 as it appeared in 1983.

OPPOSITE TOP LEFT: Another expansion of the parking garage at Sea-Tac, now the largest parking garage under one roof in North America, 1992.

TOP RIGHT: Staff monitor the airport Satellite Transit System 24 hours a day, 1982.

BELOW: Dedication of the public fishing pier at Terminal 86, 1981.

Terminal 30 with additional acreage, new buildings, and the installation of three 100-foot-gauge container cranes. Terminal 42 was augmented with a new state-of-the-art computerized gatehouse to increase the efficiency of container movement through the facility.

The Port had to pull out all the stops to keep APL, one of its anchor tenants, which wanted a new "super terminal." APL was not only the largest container carrier serving exclusively the Pacific Basin, it also accounted for at least 20 percent of Seattle harbor shipping volume. So, when the company put out a request for proposals to the ports of Tacoma, Oakland, and Los Angeles/Long Beach, the Port of Seattle worked with the mayor, city council, local business leaders and labor representatives, and various state and federal agencies to cobble together a winning plan. In the end, the Port of Seattle prevailed, Terminal 5 was expanded to APL's approval, and a great number of local jobs were saved. But APL wasn't the only shipping firm seeking more and better intermodal operations, and the Port invested $3.5 million in a new on-dock rail yard at Terminal 18. By 1990, the agency was conducting trade business worth more than $26 billion with 125 countries and was able to boast that its facilities offered Port customers "more intermodal choices than any other West Coast port."

SEA-TAC UPGRADES

Just as marine cargo volumes grew, aviation businesses were on the rise. In the early 1980s, a new air cargo center doubled Sea-Tac's cargo-handling capacity. Passenger air traffic also began climbing again. There were more new nonstop routes to Asian and European destinations. But it was the remarkable growth in feeder air service between Seattle and other Northwest cities that led to the explosive rise in airport passenger numbers. During this time, Sea-Tac's commuter/regional aircraft operations more than tripled, from 41,747 in 1978 to 150,376 in 1990. Smaller carriers like Horizon and United Express provided frequent service from Sea-Tac to Spokane, Yakima, Walla Walla, Portland, Boise, and other regional destinations, at fares low enough to compete with auto travel. In 1985, when Horizon was still developing, 20-year projections showed no need for a third runway. Three years later, traffic had already reached levels predicted for 2005, and Port and regional planners concluded that a third runway to allow two arrival streams in all weather was required to meet the region's future air capacity needs.

Nine years of further planning, studies, public comment, and controversy followed before the Port Commission, on May 27, 1997, adopted the final version of a master plan including the third runway, which then was approved by the Federal Aviation Administration on July 3. Many who lived near Sea-Tac vociferously opposed another

runway, and the Airport Communities Coalition, which included the cities of Burien, Des Moines, Federal Way, Normandy Park, and Tukwila, and the Highline School District, filed numerous appeals challenging the project; litigation continued for years.

During the long process of studying the new runway, the Port also was making improvements to terminals and other airport facilities. Having spent $40 million in 1985 to upgrade the airport with new gates, the Port completed a more ambitious $167 million program of improvements in 1992, a year in which Sea-Tac served nearly 18 million passengers. The project, dubbed "First Class Upgrade," added 3,500 parking spaces in the garage as well as new short-term parking, renovated concourses, and added more gates. With the help of federal funding, the Port also installed new surface detection radar and lighting to increase the capacity and safety of runways and taxiways during low-visibility conditions.

FEDERAL DEREGULATION AND FTZ EXPANSION

The decades of the 1980s and 1990s brought major changes on the political and governmental fronts, with the deregulation of big business continuing apace. The effects on the Port and related industries were significant. For example: the trucking and rail industries suddenly were given the right to enter and leave markets — a new factor that encouraged competition but also increased uncertainty. In addition, shipping rates would no longer

MUHAMMAD ALI

Muhammad Ali talks to Dan Whitford at SeaTac, January 12, 1984.

It was the winter of 1984 when Muhammad Ali arrived at the airport on a Western Airlines commercial flight from Los Angeles. He was coming to Seattle to promote a boxing tournament for a longtime friend.

Ali arrived "amid flashing lights and television cameras and was swarmed by members of the Northwest media who had been anxiously awaiting his arrival waiting to see that sparkle in his eye," a *Seattle Post-Intelligencer* reporter wrote. "They closed in, hoping perhaps to hear him spout off a couple of witty phrases, the kind that would make them all marvel as they have so many times over the years."

Only months away from the public announcement of his Parkinson's diagnosis, Ali didn't seem the same and reporters didn't know why. They noted his slurred speech, barely above a whisper. A friend stepped in to help with questions, something that would never have happened when Ali was the undisputed champion. Only when a youngster approached for an autograph did the old Ali surface momentarily, a reporter wrote. His childlike playfulness returned as he leaned down to the boy.

Grant M. Haller, who captured the moment for the front page of the next morning's *P-I*, later recalled that moment when Ali died in 2016 at age 74.

"He came along and stopped to talk with six-year-old Dan Whitford. They had a nice conversation and I was surprised that someone so famous would spend the time with this little guy."

Everyone would remember Ali's boxing career, Haller said, but that airport moment was what resonated. Covering professional athletes over decades, Haller wrote that he lost respect for many, but not for Ali. Haller called him a hero.

"There were no 'fake' punches thrown or selfies made," Haller wrote. "Just a connection."

be set by rate bureaus, but negotiated in the open marketplace. Rather than simplifying matters, such regulatory changes seemed to lead quickly to chaotic pricing systems with little stability. The Port responded in 1981 by establishing its own Truck Contract Program to simplify and stabilize prices, and it provided additional services the industry had long needed. The plan was expanded and improved over time, and shippers were pleased to have access to a menu of intermodal transportation options.

In 1989, the Foreign Trade Zone Board granted Seattle the opportunity to radically expand the Port's previously puny 1.4-acre site on Harbor Island. The variety of services the Port could now offer potential customers was greatly augmented when Foreign Trade Zone status was conferred on 1,400 acres of the agency's properties — virtually all of its seaport and airport facilities.

NAFTA AND INTERNATIONALISM

That same year, Congress approved a bilateral Canada–United States Free Trade Agreement, and by the 1992 presidential election, the expanded North American Free Trade Agreement (NAFTA), which now embraced Mexico, had become controversial. While some were, and remain, concerned about potential job losses, others were bullish on the idea of vastly increased business opportunities. For its part, the Port stepped up to help form the Trade Development Alliance of Greater Seattle in support of such international policies and the business it believed would be generated (the alliance also included

OPPOSITE TOP: Program of events celebrating 100 years of trade with Japan and the Nippon Yusen Kaisha (NYK) shipping line in 1996.

BOTTOM: Vessel *Asian Venture* at Terminal 30, 1991.

representatives of King County, the City of Seattle, the Seattle Chamber of Commerce, and union leaders). One immediate boost for Seattle was being named by *Fortune* magazine the "best city for global business in the U.S."

The Port was certainly doing its part to nourish that reputation. In 1992, in collaboration with the state and the Port of Tacoma, the Port established the only state-sponsored trade office in Paris. That same year, Russia — which had experienced the political collapse of the Soviet Union in December 1991 — chose Seattle for a new consulate, and the new government and the Port exchanged fact-finding missions. In 1994, the ports of Seattle and Tacoma supported the opening of a Washington State Trade Office in Vladivostok. Taking it a step further, the Port established a partnership with Seattle–King County Convention and Visitors Bureau and the state to promote tourism from markets that offer direct flights to Seattle.

That year, another Port investment paid off in a big way. The prior year, it had invested $10.4 million to triple the capacity of cold storage warehouse space at Terminal 91 to accommodate the growing apple trade. That creation of what was the West Coast's largest on-dock refrigerated storage was timed perfectly, because Japan finally lifted its 23-year ban on Washington fruit imports. Improved facilities, better marketing, and increased international outreach all worked wonders, and by 1996, the ports of Seattle and Tacoma, local rivalry notwithstanding, combined to handle a higher container volume than anywhere else in the United States except Los Angeles/Long Beach, and to handle more trade between New York and Asia than passed through New York Harbor.

THE ENVIRONMENT

Far more than in earlier years, Port growth and development included attention to environmental issues. In the 1970s, Sea-Tac become the first airport in the nation to employ a full-time wildlife biologist to control species that could be hazardous to air traffic and to promote the conservation of others. Habitat restoration projects, frequently in conjunction with other local, state, and federal agencies, were carried out as part of new marine terminal construction on the Duwamish Waterway.

In the 1980s, the Port agreed in principle to purchase the former Lockheed shipyard, a huge plot of land just north of Terminal 5 that held promise for expansion of the Port's container facilities. In keeping with its increased focus on environmental questions, the Port made the deal contingent upon Lockheed's completing both an environmental study and cleanup of the upland area, while the Port undertook a study of the underwater acreage.

During that same period, the Port engaged a new Neighbors Advisory Committee comprising nearby Magnolia and Queen Anne residents to discuss issues surrounding Terminal 91. The collaboration resulted in improvements that included the T-91 Bike Trail. Similar cooperative efforts with other community groups and city officials produced a comprehensive public access plan for the Duwamish Waterway.

CENTRAL WATERFRONT REDEVELOPMENT

While other areas of the Port were being revitalized, Seattle's central waterfront was becoming increasingly derelict. The old Railroad Avenue had been a confusing and dangerous tangle of tracks, docks, and maritime commerce; three quarters of a century later, the problem was not too much activity on the street, now called Alaskan Way, but too little. With almost all cargo being handled at the Port's modern container terminals south of downtown, only three of 16 central waterfront piers still housed maritime uses; Piers 64 and 65 sat vacant and cordoned off with barbed wire and no-trespassing signs. Along the other piers were empty, decaying sheds, T-shirt vendors, and tacky tourist shops, while small warehouses and weedy vacant lots lined the east side of the street under the steep bluff leading up to downtown. Calling the waterfront a "virtual no man's land," several citizen groups pushed for change.

In response, the Port began in the mid-1980s to shape the Central Waterfront Project. Helping guide the idea to reality were the first two women to serve on the Port Commission — Patricia "Pat" Davis, elected in 1986, and Paige Miller, who joined her two years later. The women shared a background as community activists and, with their participation, the commission began displaying increased sensitivity to community impacts, ranging from airport noise to the state of the historic waterfront.

The Port began by relocating its headquarters from the Bell Street Pier (Pier 66) site it had occupied since 1915 to a stylish building on Pier 69 (at the foot of Clay Street) — the former site of the Roslyn Coal & Coke Company facility built in 1900. Several years later, New York's American Can Company moved in and made good use of the facility's spacious 301-foot-by-60-foot dock and two-story warehouse for many years. Thoroughly refurbished by the Port, today the building houses the Port headquarters as well as a terminal for the high-speed Victoria Clipper catamaran ferries and other tenants. Port offices were dedicated in March 1993.

The headquarters move cleared the way for the Port to develop the former site of Piers 64, 65, and 66 into the centerpiece of the new central waterfront. The new Bell Street Pier, completed in 1996, featured 11 acres of public waterfront with plazas (including a rooftop park where the first Port Commission had established a park 80 years prior), a fountain, restaurants, and the Bell Harbor Marina, downtown's only recreational marina, with room for 70 boats. Across the street, work got under way on the Waterfront Landing Condominiums, the first residences on the central waterfront since tribal camps and fishermen's shanties were displaced from that exact spot by railroad tunnel construction and regrades in the years before the Port's formation.

The plazas, restaurants, marina, and condos were just the start. Development continued on both sides of Alaskan Way, and in the new century, Bell Street Pier would be the scene of a fast-growing, economy-boosting maritime business.

OPPOSITE: The new Bell Street Pier, completed in 1996, featured 11 acres of public waterfront with plazas, a fountain, restaurants, and the Bell Harbor Marina. A fully operational cruise terminal opened in 2000.

Chapter 7: **GREEN GATEWAY**

The FAA granted final approval in July 1997 for the third runway at Seattle-Tacoma International Airport. Preliminary work began soon thereafter, but construction was delayed several times by the Airport Communities Coalition's pending legal challenges; another decade would pass before the runway opened. As the first work began on the runway, one of the final components of the Port's central waterfront development was being completed. The World Trade Center Seattle opened in October 1998 across Alaskan Way from the Bell Harbor Marina and Conference Center at Pier 66. It was comprised of two commercial office towers and a Port-owned building housing trade organizations and providing a venue for trade and business development meetings. The new complex was one of the venues where the World Trade Organization (WTO) met in Seattle in late 1999. Port commissioners joined with city and state officials to welcome the WTO conference as an opportunity to showcase the region's trade prospects on an international stage, but things did not turn out quite as planned.

OPPOSITE: Opened in May 2005, Sea-Tac's Central Terminal once again gives passengers a dramatic view of the airfield. This new 240,000 square-foot "heart of the airport" has seating and tables for 500 travelers and is encircled by more than 40,000 square feet of concessions.

Norwegian Star moors at Bell Street Pier Cruise Terminal, 2006. In 2010, six cruise lines homeported 11 ships in Seattle, with weekly sailings to Alaska.

As the new millennium began, the Port took major steps toward developing the shoreside infrastructure for a form of maritime commerce that had not been significant in the region for many years: luxury cruise ships. In 1999, only six cruise ships called in Seattle. The next year, the first phase of the Port's Bell Street Pier Cruise Terminal was completed and regularly scheduled cruise service began. In 2000, Seattle became homeport to ships from Norwegian Cruise Line Holdings and Royal Caribbean International, and total cruise ship calls increased to 36. That was just the beginning: Phase Two was completed in 2001, and the numbers of ship calls and passengers continued to grow through the decade, generating thousands of jobs and pumping nearly $2 million per homeport ship call into the regional economy. The rapid growth in cruise ship traffic also raised concerns over water and air pollution that the Port had to address.

In February 2001, the Nisqually earthquake shattered the control tower at Sea-Tac and damaged airport offices and some marine terminals, requiring significant repair work. Then the deadly terrorist attacks of September 11, 2001, brought air travel to a temporary, shocked standstill. At the Port of Seattle, like all agencies responsible for airports, seaports, and other vulnerable transportation infrastructure, the 9/11 attacks were quickly followed by major new security initiatives.

TWO INTERNATIONAL TRADE CONFERENCES, TWO DIFFERENT OUTCOMES

Establishing and maintaining strong trade relationships is critical for Washington, where one in three jobs is dependent on trade. In recent decades the Port of Seattle has been a leader on this front, and helped host trade conferences that drew trade ministers and heads of state from across the globe.

APEC 1993

In November 1993, Seattle hosted the Asia-Pacific Economic Cooperation (APEC) conference, highlighting the region and its burgeoning prospects for international trade. President Bill Clinton drew global attention to the meeting when he invited leaders of the other Pacific Rim APEC nations to join him at the annual conference, usually only attended by lower-level officials. Clinton presided at a trade summit in the Native American-style long house at Blake Island State Park, a short boat ride from the Seattle waterfront, with Chinese President Jiang Zemin, Japanese Prime Minister Morihiro Hosokawa, and 11 other heads of state.

More than 3,000 reporters covered the talks, giving Seattle invaluable exposure on the international stage. The weeklong conference established what Clinton called a "framework of cooperation" as participants worked to liberalize international trade and investment by reducing regulations affecting them — a goal that then seemed relatively uncontroversial. Writing two years later, author Dick Paetzke suggested that for some, "this prestigious event established that Seattle has bright prospects as a new Geneva, an international crossroads where government, enterprise and people of good will can meet to work things out in concord."

Things did not always work out that way: Despite APEC's accomplishments, concord proved harder to find when the WTO met in Seattle six years later.

WTO 1999

Delegates from the 135 member countries of the World Trade Organization (WTO) met at the Washington State Convention & Trade Center from November 30 to December 3, 1999, intending to finalize an agenda for further expansion of international trade. From the outset there was little agreement in the convention center or on the streets, and the ensuing "battle in Seattle" did nothing to boost either prospects for trade or the city's image.

With major corporations like Boeing, Microsoft, and Weyerhaeuser, the state's large agricultural sector, and numerous small businesses all heavily dependent on international markets, there was strong support for the WTO and its efforts to reduce trade barriers. Port Commissioner

Patricia Davis, the president of the nonprofit Washington Council on International Trade, initiated the successful effort to host the WTO with strong support from her former commission colleague, Seattle Mayor Paul Schell, Washington Governor Gary Locke, Boeing CEO Phil Condit, Microsoft CEO Bill Gates, and many other organizations, elected officials and businesses.

Though labor unions and some environmental groups participating on the steering committee disagreed with the WTO's agenda, they nevertheless backed the plan to host the meeting. Many groups with deep roots in the region condemned the WTO for favoring corporate interests over social and environmental concerns. Even the longshore workers from Seattle's ILWU Local 19, despite the trade-dependent nature of their own jobs, joined fellow union members to march against the WTO on the conference's opening day, November 30, 1999.

Seattle authorities responsible for security appeared completely unprepared for the huge crowds of protestors that filled downtown early that morning, when thousands of nonviolent protestors accomplished their well-publicized goal by temporarily shutting down the WTO, forcing cancellation of opening ceremonies. An estimated 50,000 protestors organized by the AFL-CIO made the anti-WTO protest one of the largest in Seattle's history. A group of 100 or fewer smashed windows and sprayed graffiti. Police responded with a massive show of force, turned much of the retail core into a "no protest zone" for the duration of the conference, and arrested hundreds there the next day.

The conference ended without reaching the agreement it had been called to achieve because of two insurmountable hurdles—protective farm policies in Europe, Japan and the U.S., and unfair trade practices between wealthy industrialized nations and smaller, less-developed countries. The WTO continues to try to resolve these issues.

While some felt the protests and police response may have tarnished the City of Seattle's image, the Port of Seattle's ongoing interest in trade development activity has firmly established it as an influential voice on international trade.

ABOVE: President Bill Clinton joins Port Commissioner Patricia Davis, right, at a presentation on international trade during the WTO convention, 1999.

THE 9/11 RESPONSE

The call was made at 9:42 a.m. Eastern Standard Time, less than an hour after two hijacked airplanes crashed into the North Tower of the World Trade Center in New York: Close all North American airspace, and immediately land all domestic flights.

ABOVE AND OPPOSITE: Heightened security measures would become a new reality after 9/11.

It was the only time in American history such an order was made.

The Space Needle, Microsoft's campus, the U.S. courthouse downtown, Amtrak trains, the State Capitol, shopping malls – all shut down. At the airport, passengers weren't sure what would happen next. One called his colleagues in New Jersey. From their office, they could see the smoke billowing over Manhattan.

A Port of Seattle employee stood in a red traffic vest in the middle of the terminal as an informal information service. In all, 119 planes were stranded. "It's unprecedented," the employee, Richard Laris, said that day. "The airplanes aren't going anywhere."

Only a day before, Port of Seattle officials had announced plans for a major expansion. Plans called for a second terminal, a new central terminal, an airport hotel, a new passenger transport system, a new control tower, and a new main terminal parking garage. Some of the ideas captured in the plans can be traced back to at least 1973.

Using commercial aircraft in a terrorist attack was unprecedented and the aviation industry wasn't sure what the long-term effect might be. Since the airport's plan was just kicking off in the face of this uncertainty, it needed to be revisited. Though some parts of major expansion – most notably the third runway and Central Terminal – were later completed, the overall plan changed significantly, new hires assigned to the project were let go, and almost no one outside of Port staff remembers the September 10th announcement for the new plan or the fanfare that lasted less than a day.

When the planes hit the World Trade Center, the nation's major airport directors were at a conference in Montreal, Canada. It was clear to each, including Airport Managing Director Mark Reis, that the focus would be on ongoing security. Screening had started at the airport in the 1970s, with more than 50 closed-circuit cameras monitoring the terminals, parking garages, and exits. The airport introduced metal detectors and X-ray machines more than a year before it was required by law in 1974. The first bomb-sniffing dog, "No Doze," joined Port of Seattle Police in 1977, and the Puget Sound Joint Terrorism Task Force was formed in partnership with the FBI the year before the 9/11 attacks.

This, however, was just the start. Airport and airline spokespeople acknowledged from that first day that the terrorist attacks fundamentally changed airline travel forever.

Following September 11th, the airport hired a new security director to handle the daily routines and ensure new construction aligned with federal rules. On the seaport side, the Coast Guard and U.S. Customs Service worked with a new Port security director to increase safety measures, such as a four-day notice for ships entering U.S. ports.

Instead of the two operational baggage-checking systems, the airport needed eight. The problem was there was no space. So, airport staff blocked access to 2,600 parking spaces, or about 20 percent of capacity in the eight-story garage, and took another 300 feet of terminal space to help with security. That urgency led to a security redesign.

National Guard units were called. The President asked the nation's governors to use those units as stopgap assistance while the federal government put together a long-term plan to safeguard airports.

"My first priority is the safety of the traveling public," Governor Gary Locke told reporters. "I want people to feel comfortable and confident when going through our airports and flying on our planes." But even the governor wasn't exactly sure what that would look like. When air travel finally restarted the afternoon of September 13th, Delta Flight 528 was the first of about 15 flights to take off and it brought cheers from airport staff.

Some longtime practices disappeared as travel slowly returned. Non-ticketed passengers could no longer go to the gates. The Transportation Security Administration (TSA) was created on November 19th, setting in place the more-specific search guidelines that are now standard.

Reis said maybe his most significant day at the airport came the night TSA announced new limits for carry-on liquids. He called an emergency staff meeting at 11 p.m. Most of the passengers who would be flying only hours later were sleeping and Port staff had to figure out how to break the news. Every available Port employee, whether they worked at the airport or not, was called to help with lines that stretched to the far corners of the parking garage.

With everyone pitching in, those long lines didn't last like they did at other major airports. Staff avoided a major disaster and Reis saw significantly shorter lines by the end of that first day. Within a week, travelers had adjusted.

In 2023, the airport's five security checkpoints were used by a record number of travelers – 15.3 million traveling from June through August. That number included the busiest day in the history of the airport when 73,651 outbound travelers passed through security and more than 198,000 travelers (departing, arriving, and connecting) passed through the airport. Those big numbers led to projections that the Port will surpass pre-pandemic annual passenger totals.

"Seattle is on the map for guests from around the world," SEA Airport Managing Director Lance Lyttle said after the record-setting summer. "We could have done none of this without the hard work of our SEA airport team, our airline partners, partners at the Transportation Security Administration, U.S. Customs and Border Protection, and our airport dining and retail operators. They all went above and beyond to make the guest experience five-star."

Changes in security measures were most visible to the public in the passenger screening lines at the airport, but over the next several years, significant changes and new expenditures were required at both the airport and seaport. Design for the expansion of Sea-Tac's passenger terminal, in progress since 1996, was revised to accommodate new security procedures and screening equipment, adding to the cost of the project. Enhancing security across the sprawling seaport facilities posed different challenges. In the years following 9/11, the Port spent millions, much of it provided by federal security grants, to increase security staffing, add lighting, and upgrade perimeter security at waterfront terminals, and to work with origination ports to increase security at the start of the supply chain. Nevertheless, only a fraction of containers could be inspected at either end, worrying critics, who called for even tougher measures.

The rise of security concerns had one silver lining for the Port: The greater number of Americans choosing to vacation nearer home boosted the domestic cruise ship industry. With Alaska a top domestic cruise destination, the trend accelerated Seattle's rapid growth as a cruise-ship homeport. By 2003, two more cruise lines, Holland America Line and Princess Cruises, were sailing from Elliott Bay to Alaska. To accommodate them, the Port quickly opened a second, temporary cruise terminal just south of downtown at Terminal 30, vacated by container lines that had shifted operations to Terminal 5.

As cruise ship calls increased, so did criticism of their environmental impacts at sea and in port. Their diesel engines emitted soot into the atmosphere, not only when

sailing but at the dock (since the engines produced the ships' electric power). To reduce water pollution, the Port, the state Department of Ecology, and the Northwest Cruise Ship Association signed a memorandum of understanding that banned discharge of untreated sewage, encouraged better wastewater management, and required monitoring of discharges – and 14 years later, Washington State followed the Port's lead making Puget Sound a no-discharge zone.. In 2005, Seattle became the second port in the nation where properly equipped cruise ships could plug into power from shore instead of running their engines, eliminating all air emissions. Seattle was the first city in the nation to provide two shore-power berths. In conjunction with Seattle City Light, the Port provided a new power connection at Terminal 30 for Princess Cruises and Holland America ships specially designed to use the new technology. In 2024, Seattle was one of the world's only cruise homeports to offer onshore electricity at all of its cruise berths.

Seattle's cargo shipping also grew rapidly in the first half of the decade. Dramatic increases in container traffic were, ironically, aided by the first major work stoppage on West Coast docks since the 1971 longshore workers strike that closed Seattle and other ports for several months. In September 2002, a dispute over wages and new labor-saving technologies between the Pacific Maritime Association, representing shipping and stevedoring employers, and the International Longshore and Warehouse Union led to a lockout by the employers that closed all West Coast ports for 11 days. The subsequent cargo backups and shipping delays lasted for months after a federal judge ordered work to resume. Ultimately, because southern California ports faced a large backlog of ships waiting to unload and shortages of trucks and train cars to move containers, shippers diverted traffic to less-congested Seattle, Tacoma, Vancouver, and other Northwest ports.

The extra traffic helped boost Seattle (and Tacoma) container volume to record levels. Some shippers returned to California once the backlog cleared, but others, impressed by the Port of Seattle's proximity to rail lines and interstate highways, made the move permanent. Also contributing to Seattle's gains in container cargo were distribution centers that large importers like Home Depot, Target, Walmart Stores, and Pier 1 Imports set up in the Puget Sound area. In 2004 and again in 2005, the Port of Seattle saw the greatest growth in container traffic of any U.S. port, setting new records both years and in 2005 reaching its all-time high of more than two million import and export TEUs (20-foot equivalent units), for a total 14.5 million metric tons of containerized cargo. Volume remained high until the economic recession that began in 2008 brought sharp drops in container traffic worldwide. The Port's grain exports continued to increase even as container traffic leveled off. After Louis Dreyfus Commodities began operating Terminal 86 in March 2000, grain volume tripled in less than a decade as the company worked with the Port on significant improvements to the grain elevator. In 2008, 6.4 million metric tons of grain — mostly corn, soybeans, and sorghum from the Midwest — were shipped to China, Japan, and other Asian markets from the Terminal 86 grain elevator, setting an all-time record.

ABOVE: The Port had record-setting container traffic tonnage in 2004 and 2005, partly due to new relationships formed as a result of shippers diverting vessels to Seattle after a labor dispute in 2002.

OPPOSITE TOP: Sea-Tac's Central Terminal features a 60-foot-tall, 350-foot-wide window wall overlooking the airfield.

BELOW: A night view of Sea-Tac's Central Terminal from the airfield. The tower is used to control ground traffic, while a much taller tower nearby is operated by the FAA for air traffic control.

ENVIRONMENTAL RESTORATION

When progressive reformers conceived of public port districts at the start of the twentieth century and created the Port of Seattle in 1911, few if any foresaw that, long before the century's end, preventing and reversing environmental degradation would be among the most pressing issues facing the region and indeed the world. But the port district structure they created, combining the government powers of taxation, eminent domain, issuing bonds and more with an entrepreneurial, commercially driven business orientation, has proved particularly effective for dealing with some of the more intractable problems caused by a century of largely unfettered development and industrial pollution. Because of the size and scale of its operations, the Port felt the effects of the environmental movement early on, as it responded to activists' concerns and increasingly stringent state and federal regulations.

Long before CEO Tay Yoshitani set the challenge for the Port of Seattle to be a national leader in sustainability, the Port was working to reduce air and water pollution in the harbor and at the airport, and to begin reversing the effects of prior pollution. The Port was able to do so for several reasons. Given the nature of its mission, it controlled and often altered large tracts of environmentally critical shorelines and wetlands, often in areas subject to significant degradation over the years. And its "public enterprise" structure allowed the Port to acquire and restore contaminated properties for environmentally sensitive future development that might be decades away, when neither other governmental bodies nor private companies were in a position to do so.

As one example, Terminal 117 on the Duwamish Waterway, formerly home to an asphalt manufacturing plant, is a federally designated Superfund site because of high levels of PCBs (polychlorinated biphenyls) and other contaminants. In 1999, the Port acquired the property and, with the City of Seattle, initiated a long-term joint project to clean up the site

and the surrounding neighborhood. Over the next decade the Port removed contaminated soil, asphalt, oil, pipes, underground storage tanks, and debris from the site and offshore intertidal zone while working with the city, the community, and the federal Environmental Protection Agency (EPA) to prepare a comprehensive long-term clean-up plan for the area.

In 2001, when the EPA designated the entire Duwamish Waterway as a Superfund site, the Port's substantial property holdings (including much of the waterway bed and more than 200 acres of uplands) gave it a central role in efforts to restore the environment while retaining critical water-dependent businesses along the river. Although a federally mandated cleanup was not scheduled to begin until 2012, in 2008 the Port, with input from the city, Washington State Department of Ecology, local businesses, and community groups, began work on the Lower Duwamish River Habitat Conservation Plan. Adopted by the Port Commission in 2009, the plan identified 31 separate restoration project sites, comprising nearly 70 acres (approximately 30,000 lineal feet of shoreline) of new habitat. Even before then, the Port had (with an assist from the U.S. Army Corps of Engineers, Fish and Wildlife Service, and EPA) implemented considerable habitat enhancement efforts along the Duwamish aimed at promoting salmon recovery and improved refuge and feeding opportunities for wildlife.

To construct the third runway at Sea-Tac Airport, the Port needed to relocate a portion of Miller Creek near the airport, fill 13.46 acres of wetlands, and temporarily disturb another acre of wetland. To compensate, the Port restored and improved 102 acres of forested wetlands and provided fish habitat in the highly urbanized area next to the busy airport, in the midst of runway construction. The Port also selected a site on the Green River in Auburn to provide 65 acres of waterfowl habitat (which could not be created at or near the airport because of the hazard of aircraft striking birds). Mitigation work, mostly between 2004 and 2006, was followed by a planned 15-year monitoring program.

The Port also has been in the forefront of work to promote cleaner fuel and reduce air pollution and greenhouse gas emissions from trucks, ships, and machinery at the seaport, and to cut emissions and improve air quality at the airport. Since 1998, maintenance at the more than 60 acres of Port parks and public access sites has been 100 percent organic. Back in the 1970s, Sea-Tac was the nation's first airport to employ a full-time wildlife biologist to manage wildlife and habitat to minimize bird hazards, protecting both travelers and wildlife. Starting in 2007, the wildlife management staff teamed with University of Illinois researchers on a demonstration site for avian radar, making Sea-Tac the first airport in the country to use an advanced new tracking system with real-time displays of bird activity. Also at Sea-Tac, the Port designed and implemented an award-winning program that recycles nearly one quarter of the airport's total waste and introduced coordinated waste collection from arriving airplanes, promoting recycling while reducing emissions from multiple trash pickups.

ACCOUNTABILITY AND SUSTAINABILITY

Sea-Tac Airport opened its first major new terminal facility in 30 years on June 15, 2004. Along with the integrated baggage and security systems designed after 9/11 (and among the first such systems in the country), the new Concourse A and south terminal expansion added 14 gates and four baggage carousels. The new facility also displayed major public artworks and impressive architecture. The new Central Terminal, which opened in May 2005, featured a 60-foot-tall, 350-foot-long glass wall, which offered a panoramic view of takeoffs and landings. The terminal also featured 20 new restaurants and shops for passengers, all operating under the Port's new "street pricing" policy, which limited prices at airport concessions to amounts charged by the same or comparable businesses outside the airport.

In 2004, the state Supreme Court rejected most of the legal challenges to the third runway, and on August 19 of that year the Airport Communities Coalition withdrew its remaining appeals, allowing construction to resume. Although the coalition failed to stop the project, its long-term opposition coincided with increased regulatory controls of environmental mitigation, including improved quality of fill dirt, state-of-the-art storm water treatment, relocation of a salmon-spawning stream, and creation or enhancement of wetlands. More than 13 million cubic yards of fill were delivered (another 3 million cubic yards came from on-site excavation) to build up a plateau held in place by three huge retaining walls (the largest is 1,430 feet long and 130 feet high, the tallest of its kind in North America). The 8,500-foot-long, 150-foot-wide, 17-inch-deep concrete runway constructed on this plateau opened on November 20, 2008.

Controversy over the runway did not end when the litigation did. In December 2007, a state auditor's report of the Port's capital program claimed the Port had wasted millions in construction contracts, mostly related to the third runway, and called its construction management "vulnerable to fraud, waste and abuse."

The Port responded by conducting its own investigations and implementing numerous financial reporting reforms. Later, the U.S. Justice Department, which had initiated its own investigation, closed it without pursuing any criminal indictments.

When Tay Yoshitani, a U.S. Army veteran who had worked at ports around the country and had headed the ports of Oakland and Baltimore, took the helm, he stressed ethics and transparency as central to the Port's mission, and the Port became one of the few in the country to establish a Workplace Responsibility Program, including an employee Code of Conduct.

ABOVE TOP: Taking the helm as CEO in 2007, Tay Yoshitani set a course for sustainability, challenging Port employees, tenants, and customers to implement cleaner operating strategies to make Seattle The Green Gateway.

ABOVE: Crews pour 130,000 cubic yards of concrete and 35,000 tons of asphalt to build Sea-Tac's 150-foot-wide, 17-inch-deep third runway.

OPPOSITE LEFT: The Terminal 5 redevelopment involved cleanup and restoration of contaminated industrial property.

RIGHT: Port employee Monica Bradley volunteers for an Earth Day cleanup along the Duwamish Waterway.

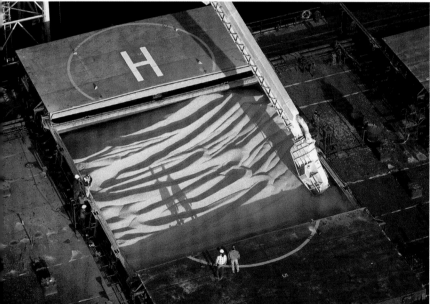

TOP: Kristi Hagen, a member of Local 98, became one of the first female "walking bosses," as ILWU foremen are called, on the Seattle waterfront, 1997.

BELOW: The automated arm at the Terminal 86 grain facility delivers grain to the hold of a ship. Terminal 86 has a capacity of four million bushels.

In addition to ethics, Yoshitani focused on environmental stewardship, which he saw as a competitive edge for Seattle, complementing the Port's mission to promote economic growth. Building on prior efforts, the Port continued working to restore habitat, reduce air and water pollution at the seaport and airport, clean up existing contaminants ranging from creosote-treated pilings to old fuel storage tanks, conserve energy, and reduce greenhouse gas emissions. With climate change a front-burner issue, the Port commissioned Herbert Engineering to analyze the carbon footprint of different trade routes between major Asian cities and central U.S. distribution centers. The 2009 study found that shipments to Puget Sound and then by rail to the Midwest produced significantly lower carbon emissions than shipments through other West Coast ports or via the Panama Canal. The Port promoted Puget Sound as The Green Gateway for maritime trade between Asia and a broad swath of the United States. Moreover, with significant and broad environmental programs instituted at Sea-Tac Airport, the title "Green Gateway" encompassed all Port operations. An independent report released in August 2007 stated that the combined environmental efforts at the airport made the Sea-Tac environmental program one of the strongest at any airport in the nation. A year later, Sea-Tac was named winner of the 2008 Environmental Achievement Award from Airports Council International – North America.

Promoting trade through Puget Sound was emblematic of the evolving relationships among area ports from occasionally bitter rivalries to regionalized and cooperative. The study of carbon emissions from Asian trade built on prior collaboration between the Seattle and Tacoma ports, including a 2006 inventory of air emissions from maritime sources on the Sound and subsequent efforts involving other ports, the transportation industry, regulatory agencies, and labor, environmental, and community groups, to set goals for reducing those emissions.

Port commissioners from Seattle and Tacoma collaborated on regional promotion and environmental concerns, as well as transportation infrastructure and port security issues. Seattle CEO Yoshitani emerged as a leader of the West Coast initiative to promote the U.S. West Coast as the optimal gateway for Asian cargo to and from the U.S. interior. He also worked with officials from other ports to lobby Congress for more funding for regional road and rail projects and environmental programs and to support President Barack Obama's 2010 call to double U.S. exports within 10 years.

TOP: Hong Kong-based Orient Overseas Container Line vessel enters port in 2004. Container lines, including OOCL, utilizing Terminal 18, operated here by SSA Marine Terminals (SSA).

BOTTOM: Longshore workers in orange safety vests are barely visible next to the huge post-Panamax cranes loading containers onto chassis beds. August 10, 2007.

ABOVE: Sea-Tac's largest airline customer, Alaska Airlines, makes its first landing on the new third runway in 2008.

RIGHT: Spiraling like a helix, Sea-Tac's eight-floor parking garage has electronic indicators on each level to help drivers locate available parking spaces.

LEFT: *Carnival Spirit*, a Carnival ship homeported in Seattle, moors at Terminal 91.

ABOVE: Enormous blue plugs provide shore power to cruise ships so they do not need to run diesel engines to generate electricity while at berth. This helps eliminate harmful emissions from moored ships and helps preserve Seattle's air quality.

FACING THE NEXT CENTURY

Growing cooperation among regional ports was perhaps inevitable given the difficulties faced in the worldwide economic downturn that followed the collapse of the U.S. housing market. At the Port of Seattle, container traffic showed the impact of recession first, dropping sharply in 2008 and again in 2009. In contrast, the numbers of air and of cruise ship passengers both reached record highs in 2008, as did grain exports. With the recession deepening, 2009 saw declines in all those areas, but in the 2010 cruise season Seattle rebounded with new records for both passengers and ship calls. The Port responded aggressively to the economic downturn, cutting costs to keep operating in the black. Acknowledging the economic hard times, the commission cut its tax levy for 2010 and committed to using revenues, not taxes, to fund future capital programs at the seaport (consistent with the policy long in place at the airport).

Despite the downturn, 2009 brought some notable milestones for the Port. At the start of the cruise season, the Smith Cove Cruise Terminal, a new permanent two-berth cruise facility, opened at Pier 91, replacing the temporary cruise berths at Terminal 30. Like the temporary berths, the new Smith Cove terminal had land-based power connections, eliminating air pollution from ship engines. Later that summer, Terminal 30 returned to use as a container terminal and expanded (incorporating what had been

ABOVE TOP: With more than 400,000 takeoffs and landings annually, SEA Airport accommodates 33 airlines with 92 non-stop domestic destinations and 29 international destinations.

BOTTOM: SEA Airport's international arrivals hall welcomes travelers with a dramatic 70-foot-high wall of glass. The restored 1928 Alexander Eaglerock biplane and a replica of the high-tech Voyager aircraft (not visible in this photo) soar overhead.

Terminal 28), serving Matson Navigation and China Shipping in an agreement with SSA Marine Terminals (SSA).

With the new third runway in use, the Port rebuilt Sea-Tac's oldest and longest runway, using 120,000 cubic yards of new and recycled concrete for the 11,901-foot-long, 20-inch-deep runway. Sound Transit's Central Link light rail, which had opened earlier in the year from Seattle to Tukwila, just short of the airport, finally arrived at the gate with the December 19, 2009, opening of the new City of SeaTac/Airport station. The Port worked closely with Sound Transit to accommodate the station and provide an attractive pedestrian bridge and walkway directly from the station to the terminal.

By 2010, the Port was well into planning for its second hundred years. Work began in 2008 on creating the "Century Agenda," a new 25-year strategic plan. As it looked to a new century, the Port in some respects had come full circle, while in others it was entering uncharted territory. Just as preparing for the 1914 opening of the Panama Canal helped drive creation of the Port of Seattle, the expected 2014 completion of a $5 billion project to build new larger locks on the canal figured prominently in the Port of Seattle's planning for the future. The enlarged canal would allow large container ships carrying cargo from Asia, now limited to West Coast ports, to reach Gulf and Atlantic ports, increasing competition and requiring even greater efforts on Seattle's part to retain its share of trade.

But while preparing for the anticipated reopening of a larger canal harks back to the Port's early days, it also illustrates that the climate in which the Port operates is very different from that when the Port was created. As noted, one way the Port has addressed potential competition from eastern ports is showing that trade through Puget Sound contributes less to global warming than do other routes, including through the canal. So a worldwide threat that was unknown when the canal and the Port were new may play a significant role in whether and how the newly widened canal affects trade through Seattle. Or, in time, the changing climate may make the canal less significant and open up a whole new set of challenges and opportunities. As the arctic ice cap shrinks, the until-now mythical Northwest Passage sought by explorers from the time the first Europeans ventured to the Pacific Northwest may become a reality, allowing cargo ships to cross the Arctic Ocean directly between Asia and Europe. How, if at all, that would affect the Port of Seattle is just one of many complexities the Port faces as it plans for the future.

By the end of its first century in 2010, the Port stood on a firm foundation. The success of its overriding mission — to use the public resources entrusted to it to promote trade and commerce, generate economic growth, and create jobs — was demonstrated by studies attesting to the Port's crucial economic impact on the region. SEA Airport, the marine terminals, Fishermen's Terminal, and other Port-owned facilities combined to directly generate almost 120,000 jobs; the airport alone produced nearly 90,000 jobs, the seaport another 22,000, commercial fishing 5,600, and the cruise industry more than 1,900. Spending by these workers, who earned $3.8 billion annually, created more than

$5 billion in regional economic activity, producing many thousands more jobs indirectly supported by Port activity. Businesses operating in Port facilities took in more than $17 billion in revenue and paid $876 million in local and state taxes, with airport businesses also paying $439 million in federal aviation taxes.

Perhaps the most vivid illustration of what the Port had achieved in its first century comes from a view of Elliott Bay at the time. The great natural harbor that was Seattle's reason for being from the time of its founding. Whether from a ferry or cruise ship arriving in the harbor or from a restaurant deck or public plaza at the Bell Street Pier, that view bears little resemblance to the dirty, confused tangle of wooden railroad trestles and small piers that prompted the push for a public port. That view, and many of the most prominent landmarks along the entire sweep of waterfront — from the Smith Cove piers

ABOVE: Terminal 46, operated by Total Terminals International, with a towering city backdrop. In 2010, Terminal 46's post-Panamax cranes handled 188 container ships and served seven steamship lines.

FOLLOWING PAGES: Seattle's waterfront, 2010. Now shifted south of the central waterfront area, cargo operations and maritime industry coexist with tourism, recreation, and environmental restoration.

WATERFRONT ACCESS

From the start, along with constructing facilities for trade, commerce, and industry, the Port of Seattle has worked to develop parks and other sites for public access and recreation on the waterfront. Before the Port was created, there were no park areas along Seattle's central waterfront. In response, one of the Port's first projects was the creation of a "public waterfront observatory and playground" on the roof of its warehouse and headquarters building on the Bell Street Pier. The rooftop park opened in 1915 with assistance from the Seattle Park Board, which provided park benches, swings and sandboxes, and trees and flowers planted in tubs.

An early port publication touted the "inspiring glimpses of water traffic and the panorama of city and sea, forest and mountain" that tourists could catch from the park, and emphasized the advantages of the playground as a place for downtown shoppers to take their children:

> Conveniently, with practically no expense, at a place easily reached by Seattle mothers who patronize the big department stores and the fresh meat and vegetable markets, the Port Commission in "preparing for Panama," also provided a new "Happy-land" for the kiddies.

Unfortunately that first rooftop park lasted only a few years. It turned out that many park visitors were not tourists or shoppers' children but sailors and their dates from the streets (giving the innocent phrase "Happy-land" a whole new meaning), and the roof was soon closed as a "moral nuisance." However, in subsequent years the Port developed many other parks and access points all around Elliott Bay and beyond.

By 2011, Port waterfront property had opened up to the public for a wide range of recreational uses, including parks, plazas, bicycle and foot trails and paths, fishing piers, picnic areas, benches and viewing areas, wildlife habitat, shoreline access, small boat marinas, boat launches, an exercise course, and more. To the north, Shilshole Bay Marina in Ballard near the mouth of the Ship Canal offered moorage to recreational boaters; a fishing pier and more than a mile of public promenade also served those without boats.

South of downtown, a string of viewpoints, shoreline paths, and parks dots both sides of the Duwamish. Port of Seattle parks also ring Elliott Bay, from Smith Cove Park west of Terminal 91 in Magnolia to Jack Block Park (named in honor of the longshoreman who served for more than 25 years as a Port of Seattle commissioner) in West Seattle at Terminal 5.

In 2020, the Port broke ground on the construction of Duwamish River People's Park, which offers 14 acres of critical fish and wildlife habitat and public shoreline access. This large-scale restoration project supports recovery of the endangered Southern Resident orca population by significantly increasing habitat critical to abundance and health of Chinook salmon. Duwamish River People's Park is located on the ancestral site of the Indigenous water-related place, ł(ə)gʷalb, referring to an abandoned or old river channel.

By 2025, an additional 50 acres of waterfront access will be added in and around downtown Seattle, including nearly three-and-a-half miles along the Elliott Bay waterfront. The 20-acre Waterfront Park will stretch from Belltown in the north to Pioneer Square at the south, and will host hundreds of new trees and native plants to support the nearshore ocean habitat and to serve as a massive filtration system for removing pollutants from storm water before it enters the sound.

ABOVE: The four-star Envirostar-certified Bell Harbor Marina is the city's only central waterfront marina. It offers moorage for 70 vessels and hosts an annual classic boat show.

BELOW: The panoramic view from Smith Cove Park spans the cruise ship terminal, downtown Seattle, Alki Point, and, on a clear day, Mount Rainier.

in the north, past the Terminal 86 grain elevator and the Port-run waterfront park below it, beyond the Port's Pier 69 headquarters, the restaurants and rooftop park of Bell Street Pier, conference center and hotel, and condominiums across the street, to the towering container cranes lining the waterfront south of downtown and both sides of the East Waterway — existed because of the Port. Add in the jetliners passing overhead on their way to Sea-Tac Airport 12 miles south, and Fishermen's Terminal and Shilshole Bay Marina out of sight behind Magnolia and Queen Anne Hill, and the physical manifestation accurately reflected the Port's many tangible and intangible impacts on the region.

Smith Cove (foreground) and Bell Street Pier (background right) Terminal handled 223 dockings and 931,698 revenue passengers in 2010. By that year, the cruise industry generated $425 million in business revenue, $18.9 million in state and local taxes, and more than 4,000 direct, induced, and indirect jobs.

Chapter 8: **ALLIANCES AND INNOVATION**

The start of 2012 came with an airport project 14 years in the making. When the ribbon was cut for the five-story Consolidated Rental Car Facility just east of the airport, it meant thousands of cars would be freed from the airport parking garage and a reduction in the number of shuttles near the terminal. The $400 million project was funded by bonds that could be repaid by a daily charge on rental fees, meaning it didn't rely on local taxes. That added up quickly when an estimated one in five of the 32 million passengers passing through the airport annually needed a rental car. Only a few days after the ribbon cutting, a Boeing 787 Dreamliner made a brief stop at the airport to test the garage's readiness—a preview of what was ahead in years to come.

OPPOSITE: Norwegian *Joy* at the Bell Street Pier Cruise Terminal at Pier 66, May 4, 2019.

ABOVE: Opened in May 2012, the Rental Car Facility served its one-millionth customer only 10 weeks later. During peak periods that year, more than 1,500 passengers per hour shuttled between the facility and the terminal.

The airplanes weren't always the main focus. In 2013, the workers behind the scenes took center stage. That year, the city of SeaTac (which developed around the airport and dropped the dash in its city name) became the first in Washington to have a voter-approved $15 minimum wage—a significant difference from the statewide minimum wage of $9.19. That initiative survived a recount and challenge to the State Supreme Court, which ruled it applied in part to companies at the airport. The political effort behind a minimum wage more than twice the federal minimum spread to cities nationwide after airport workers here put the issue on the map. At the time, it was the nation's highest municipal minimum wage.

"Voters said, enough is enough," David Rolf, president of a Seattle chapter of the Service Employees International Union, told *The New York Times* for their coverage of the SeaTac proposition that passed by 77 votes. "We have seen a national change in the conversation about wages." Three year's after SeaTac increased its minimum wage, voters statewide approved an initiative to raise the minimum wage to $11, and to raise it to $13.50 by 2020. The statewide campaign gained momentum from the SeaTac efforts.

One of the most joyous 2014 arrivals—broadcast live by multiple TV stations—was the February 3rd arrival of the Seahawks who beat the Denver Broncos 43-8 in Super Bowl XLVIII the night before. About a week earlier, hundreds of fans had lined South 188th Street near the airport waving "12" flags and wishing good luck to the team en route to MetLife Stadium in New Jersey. When the Seahawks returned with the Lombardi Trophy, the crowd that had been waiting more than an hour unleashed a roar that echoed through the hanger. Coach Pete Carroll greeted fans.

Other teams saw similar welcomes including the Seattle Storm—the most successful sports franchise in Seattle history with four WNBA Championships—returning from away wins in 2010, 2018, and the pandemic year of 2020.

There was also praise for the Port's economic engine in 2014. A report published alongside the Port's Century Agenda strategic plan showed steady growth over the previous six years including in airport-related jobs, Port-owned marine terminals, and cruise ship seasons. Airport passenger growth was also up nearly 10 percent year over year. Those record-setting trends continued.

BELOW: Thousands of 12s saw the Seahawks off at the airport, days before they beat the Denver Broncos 43-8 in Super Bowl XLVIII.

BOTTOM: Cornerback Richard Sherman, whose tipped pass against the San Francisco 49ers in the NFC Championship helped the Seahawks advance to the Super Bowl, greets members of the Port of Seattle Fire Department before departing for the championship game at MetLife Stadium.

"Port activities added nearly 20,000 new jobs to our region's economy over the past six years, creating urgently needed opportunity at a time when our nation suffered one of the worst recessions in history," Port Commissioner Courtney Gregoire said at the time. "From our working waterfront to our runways, these jobs allow members of our community to earn family wages and contribute to the economic vitality of our entire region."

For the third year in a row, Port of Seattle cruise terminals welcomed more than 800,000 revenue passengers (those arriving and departing) in 2015.

The Bell Street Cruise Terminal at Pier 66 also saw an upgrade as part of a joint agreement between Norwegian Cruise Line Holdings and the Port. The completed terminal created three times the square footage as the pervious facility and was designed to handle the 4,002 passengers on the enormous Norwegian *Bliss*, a 20-deck, 1,094-foot ship christened in Seattle upon its arrival in May 2018.

But the biggest banner headline in 2015 was the creation of the Northwest Seaport Alliance.

The Norwegian *Bliss* arrives at Bell Street Pier Cruise Terminal on its maiden voyage to Seattle, May 30, 2018. The *Bliss* was the largest cruise vessel on the West Coast and was built especially for the Alaska cruise market.

THE NORTHWEST SEAPORT ALLIANCE

For decades, the idea that the Port of Seattle and Port of the Tacoma would be anything other than committed rivals bordered on treason. Each port esteemed its independence. The Port of Seattle was formed in 1911, the first year Washington lawmakers allowed port districts through referendum. Tacoma followed in 1918. Both saw booms during the war years. The Port of Seattle started an $80 million modernization program in 1968. The Port of Tacoma launched its new facilities in 1970. While only 32 miles separated the two, battles over the years made them feel worlds apart.

When a merger was suggested at a meeting with the Greater Seattle Chamber of Commerce in 1985, the Port of Tacoma called it unnecessary and costly. Talk was raised again after the Port of Seattle's biggest container shipping line bolted for Tacoma in the 1990s, but that also fizzed. In 2012, *The Seattle Times* business columnist Jon Talton called the rivalry "historic and detrimental." He noted then that Seattle, as North America's seventh-largest container port, was largely fighting for the same diminishing business with No. 11 Tacoma.

But things turned in May 2014, most notably after nine confidential meetings between the two ports.

A few months earlier, the ports announced a plan to work cooperatively. Port of Seattle CEO Tay Yoshitani had advocated for a merger and in 2014 worked with Port of Tacoma CEO John Wolfe to facilitate meetings between the commissions. Facing competition from the Los Angeles and Prince Rupert of British Columbia ports, and the widening of the Panama Canal, the Washington ports also petitioned the Federal Maritime Commission for approval to work cooperatively to improve their competitiveness, *The Seattle Times* reported.

That September, commissioners from both ports held an hour-long public meeting discussing some of the specifics they'd been working out privately. They shared the results of an economic impact study showing a combined $4 billion in business revenue and $378 million in tax dollars. If the ports worked together, they would rank third among North American ports in total container traffic, and the $77 billion worth of goods exported

The Northwest Seaport Alliance held a ground-breaking ceremony for the Terminal 5 modernization project on July 10, 2019, in Seattle.

from the ports would make their effort the fourth-largest shipping center in North America, according to a jointly commissioned analysis.

And then what some believed was a political impossibility—the "tearing down the Berlin Wall between Pierce and King County," as Port of Seattle Commission Co-President Stephanie Bowman described it—actually happened.

On October 7, 2014, port commissioners from both counties gathered reporters and the public to announce what would become the Northwest Seaport Alliance, a cargo operating partnership merging all marine cargo operations overseen by both elected port commissions. The first of its kind in North America, the alliance became the fourth-largest container gateway and a key economic transport hub. It represented 48,000 jobs out of the gate. Wolfe was announced as CEO, and Kurt Beckett from the Port of Seattle and Don Esterbrook from the Port of Tacoma were the top deputies.

The Federal Maritime Commission gave its approval on July 21, 2015, and the two port commissions unanimously formalized the deal early the following month. The alliance was a first of its kind in nearly a century. The previous oldest U.S. alliance, between the Port Authority of New York and New Jersey, had formed in 1921.

Starting in 2016, the Port of Seattle seaport was called the North Harbor and the Port of Tacoma seaport was called the South Harbor, a renaming that Talton said, "shows how far the two ports have come from decades of blood-sport competition to joining operations." Where each port had had been competing alone against British Columbia, the alliance worked to keep jobs in Washington and to stop losing individual market share.

In the years after the alliance was formalized, the results led to praise for both ports of Seattle and Tacoma. By 2016, the ports increased inbound 20-foot-equivalent container loads by 13.5 percent. Outbound loads were up nearly as high and marked the strongest annual performance of any U.S. port.

A view from aboard the *MSC Rania* container ship at SSA Marine Terminal 18.

"Our partnership brought our formerly competitive cities together and set in motion a plan to make Seattle's Terminal 5 more sustainable and big-ship ready," Port of Seattle Commission President Courtney Gregoire wrote in an article with Port Executive Director Stephen P. Metruck. The Northwest Seaport Alliance, they wrote, was the most significant and forward-looking investment in our maritime industries in more than a generation. "With the understanding and backing of our community, the next generation can continue building Seattle's maritime industries to be the most equitable, sustainable, and successful in the world."

The pandemic in 2020 was an economic curve ball causing major congestion at both terminals. Though by February 2022, more than a year before President Joe Biden signed a bipartisan congressional resolution ending the national COVID-19 emergency, the alliance's report card was back to being one ready to hang on the refrigerators being imported.

Container traffic had increased, bulk cargo broke records, and the 185-acre Terminal 5 reopened after the first phase of its modernization program. It featured 12 inbound and 8 outbound berths. That was all good news for Washington, which benefits from the more than 58,000 family wage jobs and $12.8 billion in economic impact that the region's marine cargo operations support.

"That success is not accidental, nor is it guaranteed without continued good stewardship by port officials—as well as local, state, and federal support—to remain a viable option in the global trade network," wrote *The Seattle Times* editorial board, which reported those figures in praising the ports' partnership.

SSA Marine container cranes offloading from the *Zhen Hua* 36 cargo ship at Terminal 5.

The terminal also has the largest maritime shipping cranes on the West Coast. Terminal 5's modernization program allowed for larger cranes to reach and load ultra-large container ships with capacities of up to 18,000 containers. The improvements were also projected to bring thousands of new jobs over the next three decades.

The Northwest Seaport Alliance provides shorter transits to Asia, is the main facilitator of trade from Hawaii, and handles 80 percent of all trade between Alaska and the continental United States. With more than $73 billion in international trade, the Alliance supports 48,000 jobs and $4.3 billion in revenue.

The Alliance also prioritizes responsible sustainable growth, including reducing diesel emissions, ecologically friendly technology development, increased renewable energy, and habitat restoration jobs. In 2016 alone, ships calling on the Northwest Seaport Alliance released 764 fewer tons of diesel exhaust into the air than five years prior.

There is still significant competition, including from the southern and east coast ports using the wider Panama Canal, and from Prince Rupert and Vancouver port authorities in British Columbia, but the collaboration that formed the Northwest Seaport Alliance turned a longtime rivalry into increased revenues.

"As long as we have the 10,000-mile supply chain, both the North and South Harbors are needed," wrote Talton, a longtime watchdog of the ports' economic ebbs and flows. "They are the foundation of trade that supports 40 percent of the state's family wage jobs. . . And thanks to the Northwest Seaport Alliance, the region is in its best condition to compete in a long time."

The Norwegian *Bliss*—a ship 1,094-foot ship that can fit more than 4,000 passengers—at the Bell Street Pier Cruise Terminal, June 16, 2018.

GROWTH IN THE CRUISE INDUSTRY

By 2016, Seattle was named the Best North American Home Port by Cruise Critic, the world's leading online cruise community, and the following year the Port hit the one-million annual passenger mark. With each year came a new record: 1.114 million in 2018 and 1.208 million in 2019. That year, Seattle hosted the three largest cruise ships on the West Coast: the Norwegian *Bliss*, the Norwegian *Joy*, and Royal Caribbean's *Ovation of the Sea*—all topping a 4,000-passenger capacity.

That was welcome news to Seattle and regional businesses, too. It was estimated that non-residents spent an average of $900 with each visit here, directly generating an estimated $226.8 million in business output.

With the additional volume, there was increased focus on environmental sustainability. Expanding on the practice started in 2004, the Port encouraged vessels to run on electricity while at berth, and more than one-third of cruise ships utilized shore power at Smith Cove Cruise Terminal, setting a record number of plug-ins for a Seattle cruise season.

Even after losing an entire season during the pandemic, the Port was back to setting cruise season records by 2022. By the October close of the 2023 season, the Port had welcomed 1.778 million revenue passengers, meaning more than 907,572 individual passengers visited over the six-month season. That translated to a nearly $900 million in economic impact over the cruise season.

"Careful stewardship and planning made it possible for the Port to maintain its operations and help lead the recovery despite economic upheaval and uncertainty," Port of Seattle Executive Director Stephen P. Metruck said.

Royal Caribbean's *Ovation of the Seas* along the Seattle waterfront and Pier 66. At 1,141 feet, the cruise ship can fit 4,180 passengers at capacity.

RECYCLING AND SUSTAINABILITY

The airport's first recycling program started in 1993 and kept one third of all airport trash out of the landfill. But by 2000, the massive dumpster where thousands of pounds of plane waste went each day was a problem. To this point, the material that came off commercial flights wasn't recycled. That bugged Mark Reis who spent nearly three decades with the Port and later retired as the airport's managing director. As a graduate of Western Washington University's College of the Environment, he knew that the airport could be a national leader in sustainability efforts.

The change was relatively easy to lead, Reis said. They brought in a second large dumpster and shared a simple message to the airlines: recycling was free and dumping garbage would cost you.

The change didn't take long, and the cameras to make sure people didn't cheat helped, too.

Flight attendants were pivotal in making the transition, Reis said. Witnessing firsthand the quantity of magazines, newspapers, bottles, and other recyclable materials trashed daily, they also wanted to see a change. Alaska Airlines, the largest airline at the airport, even promoted recycling.

Additional security measures after 9/11 brought added waste, such as the bottles overflowing from garbage cans, as well as provided another opportunity for the airport to lead. The Port hired a consulting firm to assess the airport's recycling program. With that consultant and an outside grant, the airport revamped its program, hired recycling coordinators, and added bottle collection areas. The recycling tonnage increased by 900 percent between 2001 and 2005. By 2005, the airport was recycling as much in one month as it had previously been recycling in one year. The amount of coffee grounds alone jumped to 12 tons a month, and the coffee compost was used in the airport's landscaping. The organic cooking oil from airport restaurants was also sold to produce biodiesel, and still is today.

Similar to the trash dumpster concept for commercial flight waste and recycling, a recycling program was rolled out to airport stores and restaurants with the 2005 terminal and food court renovation. The following year

the airport Food Donation Program was launched. More than 500 pounds of unopened salads, sandwiches, and pastries were donated in the first week.

The efforts to help the environment helped the bottom line, too. The space on the side of recycling bins was sold to advertisers and dump savings reached six figures within the first years.

Today, the Port is well on its way to having the greenest and most energy-efficient airport in the country. But sustainability efforts weren't limited to the recycling program. The Port's environmental overview included addressing cruise ship emissions, waterway cleanup, air quality, airport noise, habitat restoration, water quality, wildlife management, and energy efficiency.

When the third runway project started construction in 2004, the area west of the airport showed the effects of decades of human activity. The Port worked with the Washington Department of Ecology and U.S. Army Corps of Engineers to introduce acres of new wetlands, thousands of native plants, and creek restoration. Knowing that some wetland efforts fail, the Port removed fish barriers, added creek enhancements including logs for habitats and plants for shade, and continued ongoing maintenance. Nearly two decades after the restoration efforts began, the fully mature wetlands and thriving vegetation endured, protected by a covenant preventing future development.

"This success at the airport shows that conscientious development can be an impetus for building a better environment," said Gordon White, Department of Ecology Shorelands & Environmental Assistance program manager.

In July 2013, the airport launched a preconditioned air network that pumped treated air from a central plant directly into passenger jets. Within a month, more than a third of the gates were using it, and the system reduced fuel consumption by up to 100 gallons each stopover because planes didn't have to supply their own energy. The process was half-funded by a federal grant, all gates were part of the network by that year's end, and the airport became the largest airport in the U.S. to supply every gate with the preconditioned air, saving both fuel costs and reducing air quality impacts on the environment.

By the time Reis retired in 2016, the airport had recycled more than 1,300 tons of material annually. When the North Satellite Modernization Project was completed in 2021, 76 percent of construction waste—20,000 tons—was diverted from landfills. Rainwater was harvested to flush toilets, ceiling construction used beechwood sourced from responsibly managed forests, the concourse was heated by renewable natural gas, and the airport had silver certification from the U.S. Green Building Council.

In 2019, the Port completed installation of a solar array on its Pier 69 headquarters, designed to annually save the energy equivalent of 10 average U.S. homes. The Port also launched an ambitious plan that year to bring 100 percent clean energy to maritime uses on Seattle's waterfront. Done in cooperation with Seattle City Light, the effort is the foundation for meeting the Port's goals of carbon neutral Port operations and an 8 percent carbon reduction for vessels and tenant operations by 2050.

The efforts around reducing the Port's carbon footprint were years in the making. In fall 2014, SEA was recognized as the first airport in North America to be certified for reducing carbon emissions in a worldwide independent program. That year, SEA also led the way with the most electric vehicle chargers of any North American airport.

In 2020, SEA became the nation's first airport to utilize thermal renewable natural gas to heat the airport terminal, a low-carbon natural gas alternative produced from landfill waste. This switch from higher carbon fossil fuels to renewable-waste-derived fuel enabled the Port to reduce its carbon emissions by 50 percent in 2021, a goal that was originally set for 2030.

By 2022, there was a 50.23 percent reduction in carbon emissions for facilities owned and operated by the Port of Seattle, also known as the Green Gateway, for its commitment to environmental leadership and award-winning environmental programs. There also were efforts to accelerate the deployment of zero greenhouse gas emission cruise ships between Washington, Alaska, and British Columbia.

That same year, the Port installed a fish passage culvert along the restored Miller Creek and developed the Port Sustainable Shorelines program at SEA to build coastal resilience, advanced the Lower Duwamish Waterway cleanup, and became the first port in the nation to purchase renewable gas to heat airport facilities.

Sustainability programs meant investing in people, too. In 2023, the Port supported the green jobs startup effort of the Duwamish Valley

Community Equity Project and increased port-related career pathways through initiatives such as the Maritime High School, the Youth Career Launch Program, and Construction Trades Pre-Apprenticeship Training. Nearly $18 million was allocated for environmental stewardship, and nearly $20 million was invested in community programs.

"Our progress requires constant visioning, evaluation, collaboration, and innovation," said Senior Director for Environment, Sustainability and Engineering Sandra Kilroy. "I am continually heartened by the skill and commitment of our employees and of our partners to make a difference and to create a clean future for people and our planet."

LEFT: The airport's recycling program has grown each year since its start in 1993.

CENTER: Shown here in 2023, the Duwamish River People's Park and Shoreline Habitat (DRPP) was transformed from an industrial site know as Terminal 117 into a 14-acre habitat and public access site.

TOP: Solar array atop Pier 69, 2019.

BOTTOM: Electric vehicle charging stations, 2023.

A REGIONAL APPROACH TO TRANSPORTATION

By 2016, SEA had become the nation's ninth busiest airport—up from 16th in 2010—the Northwest Seaport Alliance was one of the largest cargo gateways in North America, and Seattle boasted the largest and fastest growing cruise business on the West Coast. Ports cannot operate and serve customers without efficient ways to get there, and regional transportation was top of mind for the Port, particularly around building for the future. Polls consistently showed that transportation and travel times were the biggest pre-pandemic concern for travelers. On the maritime side, hundreds of millions in revenue depended on efficient transportation. With cruise seasons growing ever larger, efficiency was essential there, too.

The same way that airport design in the 1940s affected generations to come, the decisions made by modern Port leaders would shape regional transportation for decades. They had to get it right, even when decisions were not popular or the economic implications behind them were not well publicized. This was most pronounced in 2016 when what seemed like a vocal majority wanted a block of Occidental Avenue South vacated to make way for a new basketball and hockey arena. The move was expected to return an NBA franchise to Seattle after Howard Schultz and the Sonics' ownership group sold the team to an investment group headed by Oklahoma City businessman Clay Bennett who then moved the team in 2008.

An investment group led by hedge fund manager and longtime Sonics fan Chris R. Hansen spent more than $100 million for properties at First Avenue South and South Holgate Street, just south of the baseball and football stadiums. The group reached a purchase agreement with the NBA, held public rallies to bring back the Sonics, and outlined how the 19,000-seat arena would be 100 percent privately funded. The Sodo transportation concerns seemed to take a backseat to sports fans' fever to bring back the Sonics.

Port commissioners focused on the jobs, environmental impact, and economic development they believed would be in jeopardy if another stadium joined the football and baseball stadiums in Seattle's Sodo neighborhood, an area essential for terminal access.

Advocating against the Sodo arena wasn't an argument against the Sonics or pro sports, Commission President John Creighton said at the time. It was an effort to preserve limited space and access for Port facilities, along with following responsible environmental stewardship. "The Port of Seattle wants to help bring the Sonics back," he said. "We are ready to assist the city and other partners in evaluating the feasibility of KeyArena."

The last major construction hurdle was authorization by the City Council to vacate the block of Occidental Avenue South running through the middle of the proposed arena site. Port commissioners and labor unions opposed it because of the traffic problems it was expected to bring to an already-congested area. "We can't move our beautifully deep waterfront, meaning our naturally deep harbor, but a sports arena could be seated in another area," Port Commissioner Courtney Gregoire said at a packed public hearing. The decisions made that year would affect regional transportation for decades.

On May 2, 2016, after multiple local TV stations cut into regular programing to broadcast the decisive vote, the City Council made a surprise 5-4 decision against giving up Occidental Avenue South, effectively killing the Sodo arena effort. The "No" votes were cast by Kshama Sawant, M. Lorena González, Debora Juarez, Lisa Herbold, and Sally Bagshaw. Bagshaw had worked for a month to secure her colleagues' opposition. Bagshaw cited the Port's transportation concerns and encouraged a renovation of KeyArena at Seattle Center instead.

In September 2018, the Seattle City Council unanimously approved lease and development agreements that allowed The Seattle Arena Company, including the Oak View Group, to demolish parts of the existing KeyArena and construct an almost-new facility, other than the building's roof and parts that had historical designation. Groundbreaking happened on December 5, 2018. The building reopened as Climate Pledge Arena on October 22, 2021. The Kraken, Seattle's NHL expansion team, played their first home game the following day. The arena, with seating capacities up to 18,300, was constructed at a $1.15 billion cost from private funds, nearly double what Oak View Group had anticipated. Climate Pledge reopened without an NBA team, though NBA commissioner Adam Silver told ESPN in February 2024 that the league had a list of possible expansion cities and Seattle was often mentioned as an expansion candidate.

The debate around how to best use Sodo land continued even after the City Council's stadium-related votes. In 2023, developers wanted the council to loosen industrial protections in areas close to the port, arguing for more hotels and housing. Commissioners Toshiko Hasegawa and Ryan Calkins instead supported a compromise brokered by Mayor Bruce Harrell and City Councilmember Dan Strauss, arguing that housing is undoubtably a priority issue, but one that deserved its own, dedicated strategy.

Housing "must be implemented intentionally—not haphazardly—in an equitable way," the commissioners wrote in *The Stranger*, a Seattle news site. "With a ten-year plan to protect maritime industrial zones, businesses will have the certainty they need to plan and build, and we can concentrate on one of the most important issues facing the city: increasing housing supply and affordability in Seattle."

Hasegawa made a similar argument in the *South Seattle Emerald*, and on July 25, 2023, Harrell signed the new law protecting industrial lands.

TOP: Climate Pledge Arena was built in what was originally constructed as the Coliseum for the 1962 World's Fair.

ABOVE: Located at the base of the Space Needle, Climate Pledge Arena is home to the NHL's Seattle Kraken and the four-time WNBA Champion Seattle Storm.

SIGNIFICANT TRANSPORTATION PROJECTS

Many steps taken in the last quarter century set in motion opportunities for progress.

Development and growth of the Northwest Seaport Alliance—and future terminal development —was made possible with Terminal 5 truck access, completed in 1997 after $8.8 million in Port contributions. It provided separation between trains and vehicles using Terminal 5 among other benefits.

Another $19.3 million contribution helped completed truck access at Terminal 18 in 2002, creating an overpass on Harbor Island. The overpass separated trains and vehicles and provided alternative access to Harbor Island businesses.

There was the new West Galer Street overpass in 2002, as well as improved State Route 519 access in 2003, with a Phase 2 in 2009. Widening of the South Spokane Street viaduct was also completed in 2009, and a third eastbound lane from the airport to I-5/405 added capacity and safety. These were all made possible with millions from the Port.

The connection of Sound Transit light rail from Seattle to SEA—the most recognized transportation improvement in the last three decades, with $110 million in Port financing— opened six days before Christmas 2009 in what *The Seattle Times* editorial board called "the perfect gift for commuters caught up in the eternal quest to get from here to there." Port funding helped the South Park Bridge replacement, grade separation on East Marginal Way, Argo Yard truck access, road improvements in the cities of SeaTac and Des Moines, overpasses on Lander Street in Sodo and South 228th Street in Kent, and the rehabilitation of the West Seattle Bridge.

The Port pledged $30 million to the State Route 509 corridor completion, expected in 2031, and the East Marginal Way South corridor improvement planned for 2024.

TOP: Maritime cargo at Terminal 18, 2023.

ABOVE: SEA's International Arrivals Facility, a Sound Transit light rail train, and Mount Rainier, 2023.

Maybe one of the most visually stunning transportation investments was the Alaskan Way Viaduct and Waterfront Seattle program, in which the Port invested $281 million. The State Route 99 Tunnel opened the morning of February 4, 2019, nearly a decade after Senate Bill 5768 authorized $2.8 billion in state funds for the project. Within a month of the tunnel's opening, it averaged more than 70,000 daily weekday trips, with nearly 500,000 vehicles passing through it weekly. By November 2019, tolls were in place, the last viaduct piece was down, and the tunnel was a major route to and from Port facilities. The new surface streets span 17 blocks from Pioneer Square to Belltown, and the project retains connectivity for cargo, commercial fishing and cruise facilities while transforming the waterfront into a public open space and improved travel corridor, including the 20-acre Waterfront Park.

Because heavy rail is integral to the delivery and movement of cargo vessels, road-to-rail improvements were also top of mind with Port leaders. Plans to develop a new cruise terminal at Terminal 46, put on hold in July 2020 during the pandemic, called for creative alternatives that could bypass rail blockages and mitigate rail/road issues at South Atlantic Street.

Another $79.3 million was planned for roadway improvements specific to the airport. In 2019, the airport averaged around 51.8 million passengers causing significant congestion daily during peak times. The roadway had been designed in 1968 to handle about 25 million passengers annually. It was estimated that future airport traffic could have significant backups all way to the Interstate 5/Interstate 405 interchange without improvements to the roadway.

The airport roadway improvements were divided in two main parts. The first involved demolition of the fourth-floor bridge between the main gate and departures, which was completed in 2022. The second part included roadway realignment, lane additions, and utility system infrastructure improvements, with an anticipated 2026 completion date.

The airport directly supported $5.6 billion in annual economic activity with nearly 52 million annual passengers and nearly a decade of continuous passenger growth before the pandemic. What does this continued growth mean for the Port? In 2019, the state legislature created a commission to recommend a new airport location in part because, at 2,500 acres, SEA Airport has the smallest footprint of any major U.S. airport. The state commission, before a state law halted it in 2023, set a 2040 deadline for the new airport to be in place, a decade before area airport volume was expected to reach at least 100 million annual passengers.

Some of the same predictions and challenges of the 1940s are appearing again today, only with far more density and with opposition that's much fiercer.

"Sea-Tac staff are turning as many pressure-release valves as they can think up," *The Seattle Times* editorial board wrote in summer 2023. "Seattle should be proud to have such an airport. But even the nation's best can only do so much. State and regional officials need to go back to the drawing board and find an acceptable site for a second airport before NIMBYism breaks the back of the great one we have."

A picturesque sunset from the SeaTac/Airport Sound Transit station, 2021.

IMMIGRATION AND SEA AIRPORT

ABOVE AND OPPOSITE: After President Donald Trump signed an executive order suspending entry of all refugees for 120 days, thousands of protesters—along with Senator Patty Murray, Governor Jay Inslee, King County Executive Dow Constantine, and the Port of Seattle Commissioners—gathered in demonstration at SEA. "It can't stand," Inslee said of Trump's travel ban, signed January 28, 2017. "We're drawing the line here at Sea-Tac."

A week after President Donald Trump's inauguration in January 2017, he signed an executive order suspending entry of all refugees for 120 days. The order barred Syrian refugees indefinitely and blocked U.S. entry for 90 days for citizens of seven Muslim-majority countries.

Federal officials first briefed SEA Airport leadership on the federal government's plans to implement the executive order around midnight on Friday, January 27th. This was long after affected travelers had already begun their flights and just hours before the first affected travelers arrived at the airport.

Hundreds and then thousands of protesters stormed the airport protesting a handful of detentions and chanting, "Let them in!" As the crowd grew, a New York judge blocked part of Trump's order saying that the refugees trapped at airports across the U.S. should not be sent back to their home counties. The Port of Seattle coordinated with two local nonprofits, the Northwest Immigrant Rights Project and the American Civil Liberties Union, as well as with other governmental partners and social justice advocates, to ensure that passengers and their families would have access to legal representation.

Port Commissioner Courtney Gregoire, working at the gate of a departing airline, facilitated crucial conversations between legal representatives, federal agencies, and U.S. District Court Judge Thomas S. Zilly. That partnership ultimately secured the release of two passengers after Zilly granted an emergency stay to prevent two of the four people still detained at the airport from being sent back. The remaining two who had been detained overnight were also released that Saturday, including one returned to Austria.

Port Commissioners connected lawmakers with federal agencies to express their concerns and to get status updates. They also provided workspaces for their staff and additional spaces for waiting families.

Microsoft offered legal assistance to employees affected by the order; Amazon said it was working on plans to help U.S.-based employees and their families stranded overseas, and Starbucks CEO Howard Schultz said that weekend that the company planned to hire 10,000 refugees in its stores worldwide over the next five years.

Some moments were tense. At points, protesters tried to block all security checkpoints and airline ticketing. They also linked arms to block elevators and escalators. Police were forced to deploy pepper spray to disperse the crowd, and there were questions about evacuating the airport. Thirty-two people were cited and released for misdemeanor disorderly conduct, and one was arrested for misdemeanor assault.

Governor Jay Inslee and King County Executive Dow Constantine spoke at an airport press briefing that night, denouncing what Inslee described as a poorly coordinated, reckless, and un-American policy.

"It can't stand," he said of Trump's ban. "We're drawing the line here at Sea-Tac."

As elected leaders gathered at the airport, the frustration was focused on Trump's ban—something that seemed foreign to the values Governor Dan Evans had embraced decades earlier when he welcomed Vietnamese refugees.

Port Commissioners Gregoire, Tom Albro, Stephanie Bowman, Fred Felleman and John Creighton wrote that January 28th:

America is great because we are a land of immigrants and that is what made us great to begin with. As the operators of this airport, we are deeply concerned that the abrupt nature of the executive order did not allow adequate process for public agencies such as ourselves to provide service that travelers and families expect and deserve. We took it upon ourselves to request a full briefing from Customs and Border Protection to understand how they are addressing this situation. We respect these hard-working federal employees who are under tremendous strain. However, when we felt that traveler needs were not fully met, the Port of Seattle stepped up. We started providing private waiting areas for families here at the airport and connecting families to lawyers who can help advocate for their rights and the rights of their loved ones.

In September 2017, the Port filed an amicus brief with the United State Supreme Court, urging the Court to affirm lower courts' decisions blocking enforcement of President Trump's travel ban. Seattle was the first port in the nation to join the Supreme Court case in support of the parties challenging the travel ban.

Though many of the Trump travel bans continued in different forms throughout his presidency, they weren't widely supported in the state. "This ban is counter to so much of what Washington holds dear," Senator Patty Murray wrote the night of the initial airport protest. "To the supporters, lawyers, and groups showing up to #seatac to defend our democracy: thank you. Washington is sending a message."

CONTINUED AIRPORT IMPROVEMENTS

The International Arrivals Facility, which started construction in spring 2017 and opened fully in May 2022, was the most complex capital development program in the 71-year history of the airport. The new facility, an upgrade from the 1970s renovation, included a 450,000-square-foot grand hall for baggage claim and customs processing, an 85-foot aerial walkway connecting passengers from the S Concourse to the Grand Hall, and a new international corridor connecting arriving international passengers on the A Concourse. "Welcome Here. Welcome Home" was the grand opening theme, embracing the global diversity of our local residents and committing SEA to welcoming guests from around the world.

"Global relationships and connectivity make our region more vibrant and resilient," Port of Seattle Commissioner Hamdi Mohamed said. "As a welcoming Port focused on customer service, this new International Arrivals Facility brings all our values for economic opportunity, sustainability, and inclusion into one remarkable building."

By 2018, nearly 50 million passengers traveled through the airport annually. If it were a city, the 136,000 daily passenger average would make it the sixth-largest in

ABOVE: The International Arrivals Facility, shown here in 2022, includes a 450,000-square-foot grand hall for baggage claim and customs processing.

RIGHT: Performers at the grand opening reception for the International Arrivals Facility, May 10, 2022.

OPPOSITE: Longshoremen and U.S. Customs and Border Protection personnel await as passengers disembark at the Bell Street Cruise Terminal at Pier 66, September 29, 2018.

Washington State. The summer months were the busiest with a third of all passengers traveling in those months.

The last year prior to the global pandemic set records at SEA with a record high 51.8 million passengers. The Port welcomed customers back to the south side of the Central Terminal that March, completing the first renovation phase that included restored views of the iconic glass wall and five new eateries. The space also included new ADA accessible charging stations and tabletops with Pacific Northwest-inspired wood finishes.

The forward thinking of current Port leadership extended beyond the bottom line and set a model for other airports to follow. In 2019, Seattle became the first port authority in the nation to establish an Office of Equity, Diversity, and Inclusion, and is leading the efforts to become an equitable, anti-racist organization. The Port explained that institutional practices made it difficult for people of color and women to thrive and gain leadership positions, made it difficult for businesses owned by women and people of color to win contracts, and made it difficult for diverse regional communities to contribute meaningfully to the Port's decision-making processes. Port staff recognized that without greater emphasis on the root causes of inequity, it would be challenging to achieve its mission to serve all members of the public. The efforts built on the Development and Diversity Council started in 2005 and on a 2018 resolution adopting a new Diversity in Contracting policy.

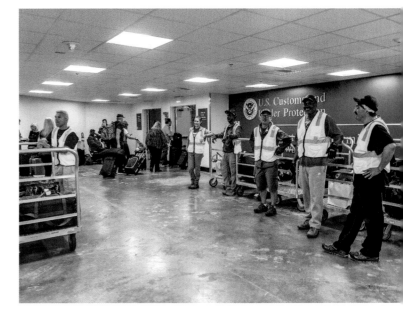

Featured initiatives included the Youth Maritime Career Launch program, racial equity training, a Commission Task Force on Policing and Civil Rights, the Port of Seattle Change Team, and the South King County Community Impact Fund, which invested $1.6 million in 30 non-profits and community-based organizations in 2022. And for the first time in the Port's history, all departments were required to set annual goals advancing equity, diversity, and inclusion in their work.

"While the Port has committed to becoming an equitable, anti-racist organization, racial equity doesn't happen overnight," Office Senior Director Bookda Gheisar wrote in a 2022 review. "It takes time, commitment, and perseverance. In many ways, racial equity is both a process and an outcome. It is about transforming our relationships, culture, and institutions."

The start of 2020 seemed normal, with Port projects and initiatives progressing. But the airline, maritime industries, and the world soon faced unprecedented challenges. In March, the World Health Organization's director general declared COVID-19 a global pandemic, and the record passenger growth SEA and the cruise ships experienced plummeted. Travel in April 2020 dropped to 259,153 passengers, where the same month a year before had seen 4,033,516. While the airport never closed—air cargo flights still happened daily, as did essential flights for travelers—it was an experience unlike anything before.

THE PANDEMIC

Authorities described it as a once-in-a-lifetime pandemic: the coronavirus outbreak that upended social norms, daily lives, and standard business practices, creating new habits and expectations on a world scale. Through March 2024, there were more than 700 million reported cases of COVID-19 worldwide and more than 7 million deaths.

The United States' first confirmed case—one that set off alarm bells and the start of the social upheaval—was a 35-year-old man who returned home through SEA.

It was January 15, 2020, when the Snohomish County man returned from visiting family in Wuhan, China, where the virus first emerged in December 2019. He went to an urgent care clinic with a fever and four-day cough. Authorizes said it wasn't a time to panic.

It wasn't, at least for another few weeks, as many people initially believed the virus was only spreading from animals to people. Airports in New York, San Francisco, and Los Angeles had started screening passengers from Wuhan. President Donald Trump suspended entry into the U.S. for non-citizens who'd been in China, parts of Hong Kong, and Macau during a 14-day period. But that February, Italy also became a hot spot and reports of person-to-person contact kept growing. A cruise ship was quarantined off the coast of Japan with passengers told to isolate in their rooms.

Then, on February 29th, came breaking news headlines. The nation's first death from the coronavirus, one of 22 confirmed cases in the United States, was a man from King County. The Seattle CBS affiliate broke into an NCAA basketball game for a live report from local public health officials, something unheard of during tournament coverage. That same morning, President Trump addressed the nation about King County's case and the coronavirus response.

While locals rushed to find N95 facemasks and bought every last roll of Costco toilet paper, Port of Seattle employees coordinated and led emergency response training for first responders, aviation and maritime operators, and federal agencies. At the airport, new steps were added to the protocols outlined by staff a month earlier with Washington's first confirmed case. Janitorial contractors were trained in bio-hazard cleaning and equipped with hospital-grade disinfectant. The Port immediately installed more than 45 new hand sanitizing stations and within a month had installed 100 more, all identified by the airport app's interactive map. Airline partners waived change fees even before the governor and King County executive limited large events.

March brought major cruise line shutdowns, including an extended global suspension from Royal Caribbean, and the Port delayed the season launch. It was a hard call: each homeport sailing created roughly $4 million in regional business activity, with a full cruise season generating nearly $900 million statewide and supporting 5,500 jobs. Even with safety protocols, the season was cancelled that June.

"The loss and impact of these sailings will ripple through the tourism industry and our regional economy—however, we understand the Port of Seattle's hard but necessary decision," Visit Seattle President and CEO Tom Norwalk said. "We appreciate the Port's commitment to re-evaluate the 2020 cruise season as the situation evolves and Visit Seattle will help lead the economic recovery and work in tandem with the Port of Seattle."

Travel through the airport plummeted. Where the year before saw roughly 50,000 passengers coming through security checkpoints daily, March had about 16,000. Several travel restrictions remained and the restaurants that could stay open did so as take-out only, a heartbreaking reality for the 20 airport businesses that had opened the year before.

However, Port employees didn't give up. In that first pandemic year alone, crews spent nearly 300,000 hours cleaning the airport, gave out more than 11,000 masks, placed 8,000 informative signs and floor decals, and gave away the equivalent of 55 bathtubs full of hand sanitizer.

They created FlyHealthy@SEA, a multi-phased strategy to ensure the health and well-being of passengers, visitors, and workers. Port websites had weekly updates on cruise travel and airport advisories, including a mask mandate that started May 18th. To promote passenger safety, the airport partnered with Sound Transit and transportation officials to provide masks for free.

In September, the Port unveiled the FlyHealthy@SEA Action Plan: a phased effort, defined by immediate-, medium-, and long-term strategies and interventions. It outlined challenges and opportunities. Detailed strategies were grouped into three parts: what had been done, what staff was currently doing, and how staff was planning ahead. The 23-page plan concluded with a simple approach: staying operational, providing targeted financial relief, focusing investment on the hardest-hit industries and communities, and aggressively implementing safety measures to support public confidence.

"While aspects of our work have changed, our vision hasn't," the action plan read. "We are a globally competitive region with innovative industries, a cultural commitment to equity and inclusion, and a recognition that we must lead in sustainability. This continues to be our path to the future."

TOP LEFT: Port of Seattle staff were considered essential workers—people recognized by Governor Jay Inslee on March 23, 2020, as essential to maintaining the continuity of operations of critical infrastructure.

BOTTOM LEFT: In March 2020, the month the World Health Organization declared a pandemic, the airport saw a 68-percent drop in passengers from the previous year.

TOP RIGHT: Port Commissioner Ryan Calkins takes a turn handing out masks to passengers at SEA Airport, 2020.

RIGHT: FlyHealthy@SEA, started in 2020, was the Port's layered, comprehensive action plan to ensure passenger health and well-being while traveling. Those plans were later mirrored in Governor Jay Inslee's commercial service airport requirements issued statewide.

The North Satellite Modernization Project started with a 2017 groundbreaking and was fully completed and celebrated in November 2021. "This event celebrates the natural and cultural richness of the Pacific Northwest," Port of Seattle Commission President Fred Felleman said. "The building embodies our values of creating economic opportunities in an inclusive and environmentally responsible manner."

The N Concourse modernization started in 2017 with an estimated $712 million budget and was completed with a final celebration on November 4, 2021.

Highlights included eight new and 12 remodeled gates, plug-ins at every gate seat, museum-quality art, a performance stage, and new dining and retail offerings. In line with the Port's values, more than $100 million in construction dollars went to small business enterprises, including some minority- and women-owned businesses.

Sustainability was also at the forefront of the airport's modernization. More than three quarters of the construction waste, 20,000 tons, was diverted from landfills. Nearly $21 million in recycled materials were used in the project. Rainwater from the roofs was captured to flush N Concourse toilets, saving the equivalent of four and a half Olympic swimming pools each year.

The N Concourse opening corresponded with the gradual increases in travel throughout the pandemic. The first COVID-19 vaccines were given in December 2020, primarily to first responders and hospital staffs, becoming widespread in 2021. Travelers were still reticent: the Omicron variant wave peaked in early 2022 and other variants peaked around or after major holidays. But SEA's commitment to passengers was being noted. In 2022, the airport earned a 4-Star Skytrax Airport Rating and was named the Best Airport in North America for its customer-centered services, facilities, and amenities. Passenger travel rebounded to 45.9 million annually.

When Governor Jay Inslee unveiled his Commercial Service Airport Requirements for the state in September 2020, many were developed in consultation with airport operators and mirrored the measures undertaken through the FlyHealthy@SEA Action Plan, a multi-phased strategy to ensure the health and well-being of passengers, visitors, and workers during the pandemic. The next month, FlyHealthy@SEA achieved Global Health Accreditation under the Airports Council International Airport Health Accreditation program. SEA was the first airport on the West Coast to earn accreditation.

"FlyHealthy@SEA embodies the work of countless people deeply committed to serve our customers and emerge from this crisis as a stronger, smarter organization," SEA Managing Director Lance Lyttle said. "It also reflects the economic region served by SEA: in constant motion, pursuing innovation at the forefront during this time of intense change to create a better customer experience."

Though the year brought relatively few travelers and the lowest holiday travel numbers in decades, those who did depart on essential work trips or other travel had the benefit of arguably the best action plan and communication strategy of any major U.S. airport.

Early in the pandemic, the Port Commission and executive director set a strategy to ensure the Port's recovery would lead a regional recovery. The goals? Keep the airport and seaport gateways safely operating. Continue long term investments. Identify new opportunities for relief for the most impacted industries and communities. Focusing on these goals would drive the eventual economic recovery.

Capital projects were re-prioritized to support essential workers at Port construction sites and the Port provided short-term emergency funds for airport and maritime business relief. Evictions from Port facilities were halted, including liveaboards at the marinas.

That June, the Port committed $3 million to a slate of community benefits programs, including a short-term youth employment program providing 220 summer jobs to those

Situated at the center of the North Satellite, *Boundary*, by artist John Grade, is a self-supported cantilevered sculpture inspired by the extending root structure of an old-growth western red cedar. The wood used to create this artwork was salvaged from standing dead trees in the Tongass National Forest on Metcalf Island, Alaska, in 2015. The fabrication of this site-specific installation took more than four years, and the installation took roughly five weeks by Grade and his studio team.

adversely affected by the pandemic. The Port also partnered with the Highline College Small Business Development Center to provide small- women- and minority-owned business enterprises with training and assistance for those interested in doing business with the Port. Ten South King County Community Impact Fund Economic Recovery grants accelerated the Port's strategy to lead an equitable recovery in communities that were both furthest from opportunity and the hardest hit by the pandemic.

While mask mandates and other operational changes faded, the economic recovery investments either remained or informed new strategies. The South King County program continued to grow, the Maritime Youth Career Launch program expanded, and the Port broadened its partnerships for reaching small- women- and minority-owned business enterprises.

The Royal Caribbean International's *Serenade of the Seas* departed the Smith Cove Cruise Terminal on July 19, 2021. This return of a passenger cruise to Alaska marked a major milestone in the reopening of the regional economy, the first Alaska sailing in 22 months.

"Thanks to the collaboration with our partners in this great city and the region, including the Port of Seattle and Alaska, the benefits of cruise tourism will be felt across the local communities once again," Royal Caribbean International Senior Vice President Mark Tamis said of the voyage, "We are back, and there's more to come."

That 2021 season had nearly 230,000 passengers with 82 cruise ship calls through October. In 2022, the number jumped to 640,000 individual travelers coming through the Port on Alaskan cruises. The new passenger volume record marked a 6 percent increase over pre-pandemic passenger volume in 2019.

At the airport, the mask mandate was lifted in April 2022. That year saw a total of 45.9 million passengers, the 11th highest nationwide by passenger numbers. SEA also earned a 4-Star Skytrax Airport Rating and the Best Airport in North America designation.

The $21.8 million, two-phase Central Terminal renovation was completed in April 2023, adding 11,000 square feet of dining and seating, including the marquee Salty's at the SEA, BrewTop Social, and the expanded American Express Centurion Lounge. The renovation project also created new job opportunities for many small- and minority-owned businesses in construction, dining, retail, and performing arts. Shortly before the re-opening, SEA marked a decade of live music at the airport with more than 28,700 hours of performances in airport concourses. SEA Managing Director Lance Lyttle, who started that role in January 2016, called the Central Terminal a blueprint of how SEA will become a five-star airport with customer experience as the foundation.

The United States's COVID-19 Public Health Emergency ended May 11, 2023. That summer, 15.3 million passengers traveled through SEA, and a new single-day traffic record was set July 24th with 73,651 outbound passengers and nearly 200,000 departing, arriving, and connecting. With the World Cup coming to Seattle in 2026 and several capital projects underway, airport staff expect those numbers to go even higher.

OPPOSITE: The full renovation to the Central Terminal was officially completed at the beginning of 2023, and on April 13, 2023, SEA threw a party to not only recognize the Central Terminal construction completion, but also a return of SEA's live music program.

"We set out to help trade and travel come back stronger and better tuned to regional needs than ever before," said Port of Seattle Executive Director Steve Metruck. "And we did that, thanks to the leadership of our Commission and incredible focus from our staff. We came back stronger."

A FUTURE OF CONTINUED INNOVATION

In November 2023, the airport announced the launch of SEA Access, the airport's accessibility program launched in coordination with a Port Commission order to make SEA one of the nation's most accessible airports through its operation and upcoming capital construction projects. That meant zero-grade curbs and ramps, bathroom upgrades, nursing rooms, suites, and service animal relief areas. This builds on the work started in 2019 when SEA became the nation's first airport to launch a lanyard program for travelers with invisible disabilities.

"There is something very special about what is happening in Seattle," said Eric Lipp, executive director of Open Doors Organization, a non-profit working to create equal opportunities for people with disabilities. "The Port of Seattle is raising the bar, not only for itself, but for airports in the U.S. and across the globe. From new curb cuts to sunflower lanyards that help people with hidden disabilities, Sea-Tac Airport is a leader and is to be applauded for holding itself to a higher standard by weaving access into its identity."

Innovation is also rooted in Port history. In August 2023, the Port Commission approved $32.6 million to transform the historic Ship Supply Building at Fishermen's Terminal, one of the oldest existing Port facilities, into a globally recognized home for maritime innovation. The United Nations estimates that the world ocean economy, often referred to as the "blue economy," is worth $1.5 trillion US dollars annually. With 90 percent of the world's trade traveling over the ocean and increasing demand for maritime services such as commercial fishing, sustainability innovations, and recreation, Puget Sound maritime industries could benefit from a global boom. The Maritime Innovation Center, expected to be completed by the end of 2025, can serve as headquarters for incubator and accelerator programs that are already helping startups and established businesses refine and scale their work.

In September 2023, the Port Commission approved a final program budget of $399 million for the C Concourse expansion project at SEA. The project plans to transform where the C and D concourses meet by adding four floors to the building's existing three with a focus on customer experience. It is expected to be all electric and fossil-fuel free.

"However, customer experience is not the only reason why we take on these major projects," Port of Seattle Commission President Sam Cho said. "The expanded concourse will expand opportunities for local businesses and support the financial stewardship of the airport by increasing revenue opportunities. The whole time we build with intention by focusing on sustainability and ensuring that our construction expands opportunities through the entire community."

OPPOSITE: The *Western Flyer* at berth at Fishermen's Terminal in Seattle after her successful sea trials, 2023. The vessel was made famous by John Steinbeck's book *Log from the Sea of Cortez*. Built in 1937 in Tacoma, and restored in Port Townsend, the *Western Flyer* was expected to be turned into a marine research vessel in Monterey, California.

BIRD MITIGATION EFFORTS

It's a short drive from downtown Seattle to the airport now, but back in the early 1940s when the site was selected, part of its appeal was the opportunity to develop relatively rural farmland. The original 906-acre purchase was home to a riding academy, farmland, some rural homes, and a rabbitry. Coyotes and deer wandered onto what became the runway space. Birds were everywhere. It was so remote that the first airport surveying crew surprised a young couple fooling around on one of the horse trails.

Planning for bird strikes wasn't as technical in those early days, particularly with fewer flights. As the volume of air travel increased, however, so did the concerns. In 1960, a four-engine prop plane leaving Boston's Logan Airport struck a flock of birds only seconds after takeoff. All but 10 of the 72 onboard died in what remains the worst bird strike in U.S. history. Another captain who'd had an almost identical experience weeks earlier described the flocks like machine fire: "I couldn't see a thing."

The birds that took down the Lockheed L-188 Electra were starlings, the invasive kind that flocked all around Sea-Tac.

Airport staff here managed the threats in the initial years, then had a breakthrough in 1976: Dennis Bulman became the first full-time biologist hired by a U.S. airport to address the problems posed by birds that live and migrate around the planes.

It was perfect timing. Shortly after Bulman started, an estimated 100,000 starlings called the airport area home. That was 20 times the number from the year before. "We have films of them taking flight in such numbers that they practically black out the sun," Port airport Operations Superintendent William D. Robertson said at the time.

Bulman had the idea to rid the grasses and shrubs of the insects the starlings and other birds fed on, and to remove the 12- to 15-foot alder trees in the area the starlings used for roosting. Three trucks packed with loudspeakers also broadcast recorded starling stress calls. Those, and accompanying shotgun cracker shells, told the starlings they'd be better off elsewhere.

His efforts were effective. While the airport had occasional dented planes from bird strikes and emergency landings, most notably a Boeing 737

that landed safely after hitting 26 birds in 2002, there was nothing close to the tragedy in Boston.

Biologist Steve Osmek, who previously worked for the National Oceanic and Atmospheric Administration, took over the airport biologist role in 2000 and the innovations continued both on the airfield and in the more than 2,600 acres of buffer around it.

When the Port designed replacement wetlands in 113 acres near the airport as part of the third runway project, staff sowed 158,000 native plants known to be unattractive to birds. That meant avoiding fruits, nuts, and berries, as well as developing a grass-seed mix with a fungus that made the grass safe but unappetizing for birds. The stormwater-retention ponds were covered in nets and lined with black plastic to keep waterfowl away from plants that otherwise would grow there. The ponds, Osmek explained to reporters, also augmented low water flow in the summer.

In August 2007, SEA became the world's first airport to use avian radar in a long-term monitoring effort to detect potentially hazardous bird activity on and near an airport. In close collaboration with the University of Illinois Center of Excellence for Airport Technology, SEA continually utilized three Sicom-Accipiter radars which functioned like powerful eyes to see farther and higher than human observers in all types of light.

In 2013, SEA also became one of three airports in the nation to create a home for bees, converting 1,000 acres into a home for half a million bees. The program was a partnership between the Port, local non-profit The Common Acre, and The Urban Bee Company.

By 2019, the Port had created, restored, or enhanced 177 acres of wetlands and buffers near the airport, including planting approximately 350,000 native trees and shrubs.

Field voles, animals about the size of large mice, live in open fields, and the airport is one of the biggest open fields in the entire county. The voles also attract hawks and other raptors that hunt them. Those birds are an added safety threat.

"There's no way that we can really teach them to avoid planes; it's not in their capabilities to understand how fast a plane is moving," SEA airport wildlife biologist Mikki Viehoever said, referring to the jet airliners that fly 165 miles per hour even while landing. "So even if they [birds] detect a plane, by the time they detect it, it's already where they are."

Airport biologists try humane scare tactics, including pyrotechnic launchers and visual deterrents, but over time hawks become accustomed to them. In 2001, the airport started a raptor strike-avoidance program that humanely catches raptors and relocates them by shuttle bus about 80 miles north to Skagit County. Those transports can happen every few hours any day of the year, at no cost through a Port agreement.

Raptor biologist Bud Anderson weighed and measured each of the raptors relocated from the airport. That information and additional data points were sent to labs so biologists around the world can benefit from the data. It also helps track where the raptors go, how long they live, and if they ever return to the airport. Data from relocated birds have shown that some have gone north to Canada and even some as far south as Sacramento, California.

In the first 13 years of the raptor relocation program, 686 birds were humanely trapped, tagged, and relocated. Only seven returned to the airport.

"It's always a thrill to see them in summer when they're 3-, 4-, 5-years-old, knowing that they've made it up here and haven't come back to the airport," Anderson said in 2014. "I think that's one of the greatest thrills."

OPPOSITE: Community and Port volunteers planting native trees and shrubs north of SEA's runways, January 26, 2019.

ABOVE: A barred owl trapped by staff along Pacific Road through the SEA Wildlife Management Program, May 10, 2019.

Today, SEA is home to 33 airlines flying passengers and cargo non-stop to 92 domestic and 29 international destinations. The airport welcomes over 50 million passengers annually and nearly a half million metric tons of air cargo. The post-pandemic growth is expected to keep breaking records.

The calls for a new airport started decades ago. In September 1977, then-U.S. Secretary of Transportation Brock Adams presented a report showing how Seattle may need a new airport by the year 2000. The airport aviation director at the time said SEA could accommodate passengers well beyond the year 2000 with long-term expansion plans. Seattle was among 10 cities specifically mentioned in Adams' report for new airports. Only Denver's became a reality with the 1995 opening of Denver International Airport on a 53-square-mile footprint that far exceeds SEA's capacity.

In 2019, Washington lawmakers created a commission to recommend a new airport site. The process drew fierce and expected opposition from land owners, tribes, and environmentalists. Possibilities included Arlington, Bremerton, Toledo, Everett, Shelton, and Gig Harbor. Years earlier there was also talk of an airport around Centralia. But lawmakers, with support of Governor Jay Inslee, ended the commission in 2023 saying they wanted to expand existing infrastructure.

As the clock keeps ticking, the crowds and the needs keep growing.

By the 2022 opening of the International Arrivals Facility, SEA directly supported more than $5.6 billion in economic activity and had set passenger records before the pandemic. Even with improvements and expansions, SEA's annual capacity was expected to peak at 65 million annual travelers. Additionally, a Puget Sound Regional Council study indicated that by 2050 air travel demand would reach 100 million people.

A scene from the International Arrivals Facility grand opening on May 10, 2022.

"It's not Sea-Tac's fault," *The Seattle Times* editorial board wrote in 2023, noting the Port's plans for $10 million in project improvements by 2023. "The facility sits on just 2,500 acres, the smallest footprint of any major U.S. airport, and is simply too small for the 45.9 million passengers who passed through last year. And because the airport is surrounded by urban development, the only options are rearranging things within the space it already has or expand upward such as by adding four stories to Concourse C."

Both the seaport and the airport were born from crisis. The region's space limitations combined with the nation's fastest growing city creates that crisis again. But the Port's story is one of innovation, gumption, and progress—handrails through each global and local disruption. The efforts are rooted in the community's values, including sustainability and equitable workforce development, while always keeping an eye on the larger vision for where the region is headed and what the future may bring.

The Port has grown from a small fishing and logging terminal to an economic power-house that manages a world-class seaport and international airport, supports the tourism and commercial fishing sectors, and has established itself as a global leader in environmental and sustainability initiatives.

As Cho and Metruck wrote in 2022:

"Though we have grown tremendously, we remain committed to our core values: creating economic opportunity for all, safeguarding our environment, partnering with surrounding communities, conducting ourselves transparently, and holding ourselves accountable."

The Space Needle with Royal Caribbean's *Ovation of the Seas* anchored in Elliott Bay and Celebrity's *Millennium* at Bell Street Cruise Terminal at Pier 66, July 22, 2021.

EPILOGUE: THE FUTURE AWAITS

by Port of Seattle Executive Director Stephen P. Metruck

and Aviation Managing Director Lance Lyttle

This anniversary edition of *Rising Tides and Tailwinds* continues a valued Port of Seattle tradition of documenting our history for the benefit of future generations.

Pick up any of our prior history book editions and you will immediately notice three things. First, you will notice how consistently change at our seaport and Seattle-Tacoma International Airport (SEA) reflects the growth, innovation, and leadership of the Puget Sound region. You will also notice how consistently over the decades the region has wrestled with the same questions about growth, innovation, and leadership.

These questions started at the very beginning for the airport. In the early 1940s, it was clear to regional leaders that the Seattle area needed a major airport. Other cities delayed their decisions, waiting for federal funding, in part because developing a new airport was not always popular – and it was costly. But the Port of Seattle, with buy-in from the cities of Seattle and Tacoma, saw the future and stepped up. The Port took on the financial burden and even selected the costlier current location because it had more room for growth, among other benefits.

Time and time again over the next 75 years, the airport transformed in step with the world around us. Known by its international airport code SEA, the airport grew as the region did. SEA stayed in sync with the 1950s travel boom and took on a massive expansion program in the 1960s that included the development of multiple concourses and the airport satellite train system, one of the first at an airport. As Seattle boomed into the 2000s, SEA opened its Central Terminal, opened the third runway, and then reimagined N Concourse into an International Arrivals Facility. Through all of this, SEA laid the groundwork for decades of master planning and development in partnership with King County, our federal partners, and the community.

The second thing you will notice when studying the Port's history is that the physical facilities are just one way that we serve regional needs. Our Port continues to connect people, goods, and ideas, particularly through innovation. That is key to our support of such a dynamic region.

Today's ambitious goals to be the greenest port in North America, to expand economic opportunity, and to provide a 5-star level of service to customers builds on the legacy that launched the Port of Seattle and Seattle-Tacoma International Airport. Future readers of this edition marking the diamond anniversary of SEA will look back at first-in-the-nation initiatives from the airport, including our Spot Saver program, Land Stewardship Principles, and Sunflower Lanyard program as inflection points that forever elevated our service to the public.

Finally, Port history books celebrate the people who imagine our future and work to make it possible. SEA Airport is a particularly special place because it holds so many personal connections. It is where families meet or are reunited. It is where many begin new lives in the Pacific Northwest. It is where visitors from around the world start and end their trips to Seattle. It is where our port commissioners represent the voices of the community that depends upon the Port's mission to expand opportunity, responsibly steward our resources, and support quality of life. And it is the workplace for tens of thousands of individuals who serve you today by continually preparing for the future.

It is exciting to imagine the transformations coming to the region, the Port, and local industries in the next 75 years. One thing that history shows us will never change is the Port's commitment to meet regional needs by investing in the future and advancing sustainability and equity values that make the Puget Sound such a special place to work and live.

OPPOSITE: SEA Airport's Managing Director Lance Lyttle (left) and Port of Seattle Executive Director Stephen P. Metruck on January 24, 2024. That day, the Port kicked off 75th Anniversary celebrations for SEA and announced a year-long partnership with the Museum of Flight to recognize the airport's place in regional aviation history.

ABOVE: In 2023, SEA served nearly 50.9 million passengers, just short of 2019 pre-pandemic record-setting volumes. The airport expected to surpass those traveler volumes in 2024. "When we think about this in comparison to our first million-passenger year in 1954, it's pretty incredible to see how far demand for travel at SEA has come," said SEA Airport Managing Director Lance Lyttle. It's a great time to celebrate all that we've accomplished, look to it for inspiration, and continue to find innovative ways to accommodate the demand for travel into the future."

PORT OF SEATTLE COMMISSIONERS AND YEARS OF SERVICE

Hiram M. Chittenden	1911 – 1915	Jack S. Block	1974 – 2001
Charles E. Remsberg	1911 – 1919	Henry T. Simonson	1974 – 1985
Robert Bridges	1911 – 1919	Jim Wright	1984 – 1989
Carl A. Ewald	1915 – 1919	Ivar Haglund	1984 – 1985
T. S. Lippy	1918 – 1921	Henry M. Aronson	1985 – 1989
W. S. Lincoln	1919 – 1932	Patricia Davis	1986 – 2009
W. T. Christensen	1919 – 1922	Paige Miller	1988 – 2005
George B. Lamping	1921 – 1933	Gary Grant	1990 – 1999
George F. Cotterill	1922 – 1934	Paul Schell	1990 – 1997
Smith M. Wilson	1932 – 1942	Clare Nordquist	1998 – 2003
Horace P. Chapman	1932 – 1947	Bob Edwards	2000 – 2007
J. A. Earley	1934 – 1952	Lawrence T. Molloy	2002 – 2005
E. H. Savage	1942 – 1958	Alec Fisken	2004 – 2007
A. B. Terry	1947 – 1948	Lloyd Hara	2006 – 2009
Gordon Rowe	1949 – 1954	John Creighton	2005 – 2017
C. H. Carlander	1951 – 1962	Bill Bryant	2008 – 2015
M. J. Weber	1954 – 1960	Gael Tarleton	2008 – 2013
Tom McManus	1958 – 1964	Tom Albro	2010 – 2017
John M. Haydon	1960 – 1969	Stephanie Bowman	2013 – 2021
Gordon Newell	1960 – 1963	Courtney Gregoire	2013 – 2019
Frank R. Kitchell	1961 – 1973	Rob Holland	2010 – 2013
Miner H. Baker	1963 – 1969	Peter Steinbrueck	2018 – 2021
Robert W. Norquist	1963 – 1969	Ryan Calkins	2018 –
Merle D. Adlum	1964 – 1983	Sam Cho	2020 –
J. Knox Woodruff	1969 – 1973	Fred Felleman	2016 –
Fenton Radford	1969 – 1970	Toshiko Grace Hasegawa	2022 –
Paul S. Friedlander	1970 – 1983	Hamdi Mohamed	2022 –
Henry L. Kotkins	1970 – 1983		

OPPOSITE: Seattle's Smith Tower was under construction when the first port commissioners took office in 1911. Burns Lyman Smith, son of L. C. Smith for whom the building is named, dreamed it would be "the world's highest outside of New York, and the firm would have a cachet that would help elevate sales of Smith's new product, the typewriter." The building opened with fanfare on July 4, 1914.

PORT OF SEATTLE GENERAL MANAGERS

From 1911 to 1933, there were no general managers per se of the Port of Seattle. Following the inception of the Port Commission, Assistant Secretary Hamilton Higday performed the duties of a general manager. Managers J. R. West, Col. W. C. Bickford, and George T. Treadwell also held concurrent responsibilities as chief engineer. Later the position took the title of Executive Director, and in 2001 it was changed to Chief Executive Officer.

J. R. West	June 1933 – January 1935
W. C. Bickford	January 1935 – November 1945
Warren D. Lamport	February 1946 – September 1951
George T. Treadwell	October 1951 – July 1953
Howard M. Burke	November 1953 – June 1964
J. Eldon Opheim	July 1964 – January 1977
Richard D. Ford	January 1977 – June 1985
James D. Dwyer	July 1985 – September 1988
Zeger van Asch van Wijck	January 1989 – July 1992
Mic R. Dinsmore	August 1992 – March 2007
Tay Yoshitani	March 2007 – September 2014
Ted Fick	September 2014 – February 2017
Dave Soike	February 2017 – January 2018
Stephen P. Metruck	February 2018 –

ABOVE: Terminal 107, a seven-acre park with pathways, fish and wildlife habitat, and restored shoreline, is one of 20 public areas the Port maintains using organic landscaping.

RIGHT: Port of Seattle centennial lapel pin.

PORT OF SEATTLE INTERNATIONAL LABOR PARTNERS AND AFFILIATED LOCAL UNIONS

Association of Flight Attendants-CWA
  Council 19
Air Line Pilots Association (ALPA)
Cement Masons & Plasterers
  Local 528
Inlandboatmen's Union of the Pacific
International Association of Firefighters
  (IAFF)
Local 1257
International Association of Heat and
  Frost Insulators and Allied Workers
  (HFIAW)
International Association of Machinists
  and Aerospace Workers (IAM)
  District Lodge 751
International Association of Machinists
  and Aerospace Workers (IAM)
  Local 289
  Local 2202
International Brotherhood of Electrical
  Workers (IBEW)
  Local 46
International Longshore & Warehouse
  Union (ILWU)
  Local 9
  Local 19
  Local 52
  Local 98
International Organization of Masters,
  Mates & Pilots (MM&P)
  District 1-PCD
International Union of Operating
  Engineers (IUOE)
  Local 302
  Local 612
International Union of Painters and Allied
  Trades (IUPAT)
  District Council 5
Iron Workers
  Local 86
LIUNA!
  Local 242

PROTEC17
Sailors' Union of the Pacific
Seattle Building & Construction
  Trades Council
SEIU6
Sheet Metal Workers International
  Association (SMW)
  Local 66
SMART Transportation Division
  Local 1348
The International Alliance of Theatrical
  Stage Employees (IATSE)
  Local 15
The International Brotherhood of
  Teamsters (IBT)
  Local 117
  Local 174
  Local 763
The Marine Engineers' Beneficial
  Association (MEBA)
  District 1
The Martin Luther King, Jr. County
  Labor Council (MLK Labor)
The United Food and Commercial
  Workers International Union 3000
  (UFCW)
United Association of Plumbing and
  Pipefitting Industry
  Local 32
UA Sprinkler Fitters
  Local 699
United Inland Membership Group (UIG)
United Union of Roofers, Waterproofers,
  and Allied Workers
  Local 54
UNITE HERE
  Local 8
Washington Building Trades
Washington State Labor Council
Western States Regional Council of
  Carpenters

Union subcontractors from marine maintenance plumbing crew, members of United Association of Plumbing and Pipefitting Industry Local 32, work to maintain the waterfront facilities.

A NOTE ON SOURCES

All works of history rest on a foundation of earlier work and this book is no exception. We drew heavily on the two prior published histories of the Port of Seattle: *A History of the Port of Seattle* by Padraic Burke, which appeared in 1975, and *Pioneers and Partnerships: A History of the Port of Seattle*, an adaptation and updating of Burke's work by Dick Paetzke, published two decades later. Equally valuable for its comprehensive and detailed account of the Port's formation and early years was the unpublished manuscript of a draft history of the Port prepared around 1970 by Bainbridge Island journalist Walt Woodward.

We relied on the work of many historians of Seattle and the Northwest for additional details of Port history as well as the broader historical context in which the Port developed. The following were particularly helpful: Richard Berner, *Seattle in the 20th Century*; Archie Binns, *Northwest Gateway: The Story of the Port of Seattle*; Paul Dorpat, *Seattle Waterfront: An Illustrated History*; Paul Dorpat and Genevieve McCoy, *Building Washington: A History of Washington State Public Works*; Robert E. Ficken, *Washington Territory* and *Washington State: The Inaugural Decade, 1889-1899*; Nard Jones, *Seattle*; Murray Morgan, *Skid Road: An Informal Portrait of Seattle*; Roger Sale, *Seattle Past To Present*; Sam L. Sutherland, "Fishermen's Terminal: Million-Dollar Industry," in *Magnolia: Making More Memories*; and Anne B. Swensson, *A Brief History of Seattle's South-Central Waterfront*.

Several publications prepared over the years by Port employees provided background on various aspects of Port history. These include *Port of Seattle: A Municipal Corporation Whose Stockholders are the Whole People of King County*, from 1915; *The Port of Seattle: A Case History in Public Port Development*, written in 1952 by George T. Treadwell, longtime Port chief engineer and general manager; and *Port in a Storm: An Historical Review of the Founding of the Port of Seattle*, published in 1971 on the Port's 70th anniversary. We also made significant use of primary and secondary source documents available on the Port's website (www.portseattle.org).

Finally, we turned repeatedly to work by our colleagues on HistoryLink.org, the Free Online Encyclopedia of Washington State History, among which must be singled out the comprehensive suite of essays on the history of Seattle-Tacoma International Airport by the greatly missed Walt Crowley, cofounder and first executive director of HistoryLink. Please go to HistoryLink.org for further information and sources on the Port of Seattle, public ports in Washington, and many of the historical figures and events discussed in this book.

ACKNOWLEDGMENTS

The authors wish to express their gratitude to the following kind folks for their invaluable assistance with the production of this book: Dusti Banazzio, Nancy Blanton, Devlin Donnelly, Jane Kilburn, Katie Nowlin, Kathy Roeder, and Rob Walgren at the Port of Seattle; Thomas R. Speer, with Duwamish Tribal Services; Nancy Kinnear; Petyr Beck and his team at Documentary Media; and Tom Brown, Kiku Hughes, Marie McCaffrey, Jennifer Ott, Nick Rousso, and Charles Smyth, our colleagues at HistoryLink.org.

We also wish to offer a nod to fellow writers who blazed earlier trails exploring various aspects of the Port of Seattle's history, among them: Archie Binns, Ray Bishop, Padraic Burke, Chet Clausen, Walt Crowley, Paul Dorpat, Nard Jones, Dick Paetzke, Roger Sale, and Walt Woodward. Finally, and especially, grateful thanks to Colleen O'Connor from Kit Oldham; to Kate Race from Peter Blecha; and to Laird, Jackson, and Maeve from Casey McNerthney, for your support during this year-long project and always.

Terminal 18 is the largest container facility in the Pacific Northwest, with fully automated OCR and RFID technology.

IMAGE CREDITS

All images courtesy of the Port of Seattle Archive, the Port of Seattle Photography Collection, or Washington State Archives, except as indicated.

FRONT ENDSHEET

Bird's Eye View: Seattle and Environs. Augustus Koch, 1891. University of Washington Libraries, Special Collections, map 123

P. 6 AND 7

Aerial View of Seattle, 1878. University of Washington Libraries, Special Collections, map 119

P. 8

Coal Bunkers. Lawrence Denny Lindsey. MOHAI, 2002.3.1643

P. 10

a: Logs await shipment at King Street Coal Bunkers, Seattle, Washington, 1889. University of Washington Libraries, Special Collections bab 43

c: Postcard: Delivery wagons of the Seattle Coal and Fuel Co., Railroad Ave. S. and Dearborn St., ca. 1909. University of Washington Libraries, Special Collections, sea 1789

d: Postcard: Post card: Railroad Avenue looking north. University of Washington Libraries, Special Collections, uw 27022z

P. 11

King Street Coal Docks. Washington State Archives

P.13

map: Duwamish and Seattle Harbor, 1854. Courtesy Peter Blecha Archives

P. 14

Burning of Seattle from the Docks, 1891. Washington State Archives

Columbia and Puget Sound Railway Station and Docks, ca. 1882. University of Washington Libraries, Special Collections, A. Curtis 26436, uw 5852

P. 15

James J. Hill. National Archives

Thomas Burke. MOHAI, shs 12455

P. 16

a: Passengers on Victoria*, ca. 1904–1910.* Puget Sound Maritime Historical Society, 2635-945 and 2635-947

b: Alaska Steamship Company brochure. Courtesy Bjorn Larsson, Timetable Images

P. 18

Railroad Avenue looking north. Puget Sound Maritime Historical Society, 1741-86

P. 19

a: Reginald H. Thomson. Seattle Municipal Archives, 64766

b: George F. Cotterill. Seattle Municipal Archives, 12280

P. 20 AND 21

Seattle waterfront, looking north. University of Washington Libraries, Special Collections, sea 0649

P. 22

Hiram M. Chittenden. University of Washington Libraries, Special Collections, uw por0022

P. 23

George F. Cotterill. University of Washington Libraries, Special Collections, uw 25806

P. 28

c: The new plans for the development of Harbor Island. University of Washington Libraries, Special Collections, uw 5987

P. 30

Seattle, looking west from 1st Avenue and Yesler Way, ca. 1913. University of Washington Libraries, Special Collections, uw 9939

P. 31

a: The Great Northern Docks at Smith Cove and the Steamship Minnesota. University of Washington Libraries, Special Collections, sea 2159

b: Fishermen's Terminal dedication, January 10, 1914. MOHAI, shs 15004

P. 32

a: "Untitled Panoramic of Smith Cove," ca. 1880s, by Emily Inez Denny. MOHAI, a1955.878.3

P. 35

a: Loading Samson Brand Apples, Asahel Curtis. Washington State Historical Society

P. 36

Robert Bridges and Family. Courtesy the Bridges Family

P. 37

Launching of the ship Snoqualmie*, August 1919.* MOHAI, shs 3533

P. 38 AND 39

a: Men load silk. MOHAI, shs 1221

b: Panorama of Seattle waterfront, 1917. Library of Congress

P. 41

Boeing Plant 1, "The Red Barn." Boeing Archive, BI226767

Boeing B & W. Boeing Archive, BI22480

P. 45

d: Hooverville mail sign. MOHAI, 1980.7029.1

P. 46

b: Washington State apples, in storage at Port warehouse, ca. 1920s. Washington State Archives

P. 47

Matt H. Gormley, Port auditor. Washington State Archives

Railroad Avenue, 1934. Seattle Municipal Archives, 8991

P. 48

Policemen post behind bales of hay. MOHAI, *Seattle Post- Intelligencer* Collection, pi 24007

P. 49

Strikers block a train during the Battle of Smith Cove, 1934. MOHAI, *Seattle Post-Intelligencer* Collection, pi 24001

P. 52

Strikers at the entrance of Smith Cove, 1934. MOHAI, *Seattle Post-Intelligencer* Collection, pi 24004

P. 54

Seattle Army Port of Embarkation. Coast Guard Museum

Sailors ship out at the Port of Embarkation. MOHAI, 1986.5.10558.1

P. 57

c: Construction of the Ship Canal Bridge. MOHAI, 2009.23.57

P. 61

Strikers, 1947. MOHAI, *Seattle Post-Intelligencer* Collection, PI 24163

P. 62

Salmon Bay Post Card. University of Washington Libraries, Special Collections, sea 1924

P. 63

a: Salmon Bay Charlie. Courtesy Paul Dorpat

P. 74

a: Harry Bridges. MOHAI, *Seattle Post-Intelligencer* Collection, 1986.5.19895

P. 80

c: President John F. Kennedy with Senator Magnuson at Sea-Tac. The Seattle Times

P. 81

Lyndon B. Johnson at Sea-Tac Airport, 1966. Seattle Municipal Archives, 63797

P. 82

Seattle, looking north along the East Waterway, ca. 1965. University of Washington Libraries, Special Collections, sea, 1626

P. 88

a: Governor Dan Evans. MOHAI, *Seattle Post-Intelligencer* Collection, 2000.107.220.20.05

P. 95

Tina Mucklow. MOHAI, *Seattle Post-Intelligencer Collection,* SKMBT C55010111616082

P.100

Muhammad Ali. MOHAI, *Seattle Post-Intelligencer Collection*

P. 140

Protest at Sea-Tac, 2017. Photo by Dennis Bratland, CCA-SA4.0

P.141

Immigration protest. Photo by Josh Trujillo

INDEX